WHERE DID YOU COME FROM SUPERMAN?

BY

JACEK PERZYNSKI

WINGED HUSSAR PUBLISHING

Where Did You Come From Superman? by Jacek Perzynski
Cover design by Vincent Rospond
This edition published in 2018

Winged Hussar Publishing, is an imprint of

Pike and Powder Publishing Group LLC
1525 Hulse Rd, Unit 1
Point Pleasant, NJ 08742

Copyright © Jacek Perzynski
ISBN 978-1-945430-57-2
LCN 2018945496

Bibliographical References and Index
1. History/Biography. 2. Poland. 3. Zishe Breitbart

Pike and Powder Publishing Group LLC All rights reserved
For more information on Pike and Powder Publishing Group, LLC,
visit us at

www.PikeandPowder.com

www.wingedhussarpublishing.com

twitter: **@pike_powder**

facebook: **@PikeandPowder**

Where did you come from Superman?

1. Breitbart was also called the King of Iron

The author expresses special thanks to Gary Bart, who is closely related to the unusual hero of this book for help and sharing unique materials necessary for the creation of this work.

STRYKÓW,
FAMILY CITY OF POWER

The real-life character whose story is depicted on the pages of a novel or film always fires the imagination. This biography is more colorful than the novelties invented by writers. It happens, however, that in the film or book the fate of the hero is significantly different from what often really happened. That also applies to the hero of this book. Over the years, he has become more and more of a legend and a myth.

The biography of our hero is sensational and unique, but it also includes the bitterness of childhood, years of poverty, many disappointments and great ambition supported by a strong will - the ambition to become someone. There is also a great mission and message in its telling. It is a story about an extraordinary man almost forgotten for years, whose life gave rise to the biggest icon of pop culture today. What you must keep in mind when reading this story is not just the tale, but the tales that seem to have grown up around him

Is Superman a completely fictional and impersonal character, as we often read when searching for information about him?

Is that all there is to it?

Let's remember that in principle every hero of a movie, a book, etc. has its prototype - a person whose life was an inspiration, who provided a fascination so great that he was not allowed to disappear into the reverie of history.

It is said that it is difficult to create an official life story of Superman, a figure that has existed in mass culture for over seventy years. There is always one original, and the reader will find out after reading this book where this original came from.

Let's start from the beginning. Our hero was born in an exceptional place ...

2. Stryków lies 10 km north of Łódź

Exceptional, because it is extremely important for shaping his psyche, personality and character. This person's name was Zishe Breitbart, he was born in the town of Stryków, which today is in central Poland. This small town is located about ten kilometers from the big city of Łódź. This is the first very important note for the American reader of this book. In most English-language publications that have been written about Zishe Breitbart, you can find multiple, erroneous bits of information that he was born in Łódź in the Stryków district. We will come back to clarify this fact. The advantage of the city was and still is its location at the intersection of the main roads of Poland at that time.

Stryków received city rights[1] thanks to the Polish king Władysław Jagiełło in 1394. In the mid-15th century, Stryków had over five hundred inhabitants and was ranked as a medium-sized city. The relatively good location on trade routes ensured its development, which lasted until the mid-seventeenth century during the Polish war with Sweden. This war was so terrible for Poland that the destruction of the country it caused was comparable to those of the years of World War II! This very large state was weakened despite attempts to rebuild.

1. Rights granted to the town regarding trade and self-government

3. Today's Stryków lies at a crossroads of European highways

Reforms did not bring results mainly due to interference by their neighboring countries.

After the final collapse of Poland in 1795, Stryków was under the administration of Prussia, then Napoleon, who created the Duchy of Warsaw in 1807-1815. In the end of 1815, the town was ruled by the Russian tsars as part of the "Congress Kingdom of Poland". After 1831 this area was incorporated directly into the huge Russian state.

Stryków was a place of strong Hasidic influence. The Hasidim had their own Hasidic synagogues and prayer. They created a compact and strong environment, almost like families based on strong ties of brotherly friendship. At their head were Tzadiks[2] from various dynasties of Rabbinical Courts. This religious-mystical movement (from Hebrew, pious, God-fearing) was born in eastern Poland during the mid-18th century in the bosom of Judaism. It was created in response to cultural unrest, the decline of piety and had a renewing character. Hasidism transformed into a mystical movement that developed the form of worshiping God through song and dance. The Tzadik was the leader of the religious community in Hasidism as well as the model of piety, wisdom, justice and authority in matters of faith. Yiddish, the language of the Jewish community was used throughout the Polish lands, and in the vicinity of Łodz was spoken of as a characteristic singing dialect, which has not completely disappeared, while some words, phrases, and definitions entered Polish for good. The Tzadik

2. Righteous leader

9

Elimelech Menachem Mendel Landau founded his court in Stryków. Rabbi Efraim Izaak Fiszel taught there in the first decade of the 20th Century.

In the city on the Old Market Square there was a synagogue, and next to it a mikveh[3], as well as a shelter for the poor behind it. The square was surrounded by houses and shops, and in the middle was a well from which the Jews drew water. The New Market Square was surrounded by several brick houses - in the middle of which stood a Catholic church. Only a few squares and roads were paved. The town also contained a cheder (a Jewish religious school). Strykow's synagogue and its community popular among the local Jews. They could live where they wanted, without creating a separate district. Interspersed between the Jewish houses there were houses of Polish burghers. There were never ghettos in Poland, of the kind that existed in the Germany and Italy, where Jewish people were only allowed to go out during the day. This is a very important fact to explain why so many Jewish people sought shelter and emigrated to the Polish lands – with the largest concentration of the Jewish community in Europe. They had greater autonomy and freedom here than in other parts of Europe.

The largest part of the citizens in this part of the country was engaged in trade in agricultural and as craftsmen. The Jewish citizens were also engaged in various trades that included wool, hops, cloth, cotton and spices. In 1860, the city's population amounted to 2,413 inhabitants, of which the vast majority – 1,609 - were of the Jewish faith. Among these residents there were 65 tailors, 53 farmers and 35 shoemakers. The Christian and Jewish communities were intertwined with one another in a relatively harmonious existence. It was in this environment that Zishe came into the world.

The year that Zishe was born and later raised in Stryków was a time when Poland was not present on the maps of Europe (Poland did not exist as a state), and its lands were in the hands of three invaders: Prussia, Austria and Russia.[4] The severe political and economic situation of the people living there combined with a growing population forced active and enterprising individuals to look for work abroad. Most often the destination was the US. One such resident of the Jewish faith born in Stryków, who followed this path must be mentioned.

His name was Awrom Pinkas Unger, who in his memoir *My Town Stryków - Majn hejmsztetl Stryków* (title in Yiddish) described the life of the city at the

---

3. Ritual bath
4. Poland was partitioned three times in the late 18th century and only re-emerged for a short time as a rump state during the Napoleonic wars before disappearing again.

4. Photograph of the Synagogue of Stryków from the 1920's

turn of the 19th and 20th Centuries when Zishe was growing up there. At the beginning of the 20th century he emigrated to the USA, and his memoire was recommended reading by the New York Jewish Science Institute's (JIWO) as an interesting biography of a Jewish emigrant. It was published in Yiddish, in New York, in 1956.

It is in these memories that we can find the following excerpt at the beginning of his story: *"I remember that when I was a boy, our great poet Yitskhok Leybush Peretz[5] came to Stryków. It was Friday and Peretz asked the Shames (rabbi's assistant) to open the synagogue, because he wanted to see the interior, along with the vestibule in which shackles were located, and the women's gallery (room in the synagogue for women). It is said that he wrote In polisz af der kejt[6] in the vestibule of the synagogue"* (Peretz had just seen the stocks of Stryków). So yes, Stryków can be called a city connected to the world of literature

There is another passage in this book that is worth mentioning to the American reader concerning Łódź (pronounced "Woodz"), which almost everyone else in Poland regards as the birthplace of Zishe Breitbart. In 1784 Łódź was a small town with only two Jewish families amounting to seven people! While it is true the population grew rapidly in the following years, but the life of most Jewish people and growth of the community was on the outskirts of the city for many generations. The document establishing the Jewish commune in Łódź in 1806 lists the synagogue in Stryków, as the one to which the Łódź Jews were

---

5. Isaac Lieb Peretz (1852-1915) classical Yiddish writer, poet and playwright.
6. *"In Poland is a way out"*

subject! Giving credence to the notion that Jewish residents in Łódź had to visit Stryków to perform their religious duties. Further, it was in Stryków that great entrepreneurs intended to build their factories and develop a great industry. How did this happen?

In 1826, the owner of Stryków, Feliks Czarnecki, announced a package of discounts for potential investors - entrepreneurs intending to settle in the city. In this situation, the craftsmen, among whom the Jews dominated, played a huge role. This ambitious plan eventually collapsed in 1830, when an uprising against the Tsar called "The November Uprising" erupted in Poland. The city report of 1837 informs that due to the fall of the city is was unable to maintain or purchase streetlights set on poles in which candles were lit.

For many years, Stryków attracted interest among manufacturers wanting to build their factories on the Oceanic River - this was still the case in Zishe Breitbart's childhood. However, the biggest opponent of such a solution was not the excessive price of land, but the inhabitants of the city, who forbade building anything here for fear of ... poisoning water. The river flowing through the city was extremely important for the residents. Numerous craft workshops were created along it. Ritual ablutions (baths) were performed by Jewish residents here because many of them could not afford to use the mikvah[7], because the fee was too high. Because of this the factory owners went to nearby Łódź and built their plants there. In this way, a very small boat almost imperceptibly on the map of Polish lands became a large industrial city and kept the rural nature of Stryków intact.

It is still necessary to explain the historical context related to some of the terms in this book for the American reader. He may wonder what, for example, what is meant that Zishe, born in Poland in a Jewish family, lived in Poland as part of the Russian Empire. Well, at the time of his birth, as mentioned above, Poland was not on the world map because it was divided between three countries: Russia, Prussia and Austria. The first partition made in 1772, the second in 1793 and the third 1795. After the third partition, Poland ceased to exist. Poland regained its independence and was again established as a free state in 1918. The lands where the Zishe family lived were annexed as part of the Russian partition. This was a poor, underdeveloped land, treated by the Russians as an economic reservoir to pull from. It was, therefore, a typical province, from which only profits and material benefits were derived. In this context Zishe went into World War I as a subject of the Tsar in the Russian army.

---

7. Ritual baths.

Before the outbreak of World War II, Stryków was inhabited by nearly five thousand people, of whom about 40 percent were Jews. After its end, the community from which Zishe Breitbart originated and was so intertwined with his legend virtually ceased to exist.

Let's start the story of this extraordinary man.

5. *A section from the book,* Muscular Power

THE FIRST YEARS OF ZISHE'S LIFE

The documented roots of the Breitbart family in Stryków begin approximately in 1755 (at a time when there was still an independent Poland), in which a boy named Rafał comes into the world. Later, he marries a woman named Loja. Rafał's family started a line of butchers. They could not afford their own flat, which is why they rented a room in the homes of richer Jewish families. This is also around the time when Hasid's first come to the city. Around 1788, their son Lewek is born. He, in turn, marries Szajdla Abramowicz. Their son is Abram, married Taube Wilk, also from family of butchers. In 1843 their son Gerszon is born, and his wife is Taube Fajgla Kujawski. One year after the wedding, in 1862, Icek Hersz is born, who later lived with Zelda Gitla Testylier, who was one year younger than himself. Icek was the first man in the family who did not become a butcher, but instead became a blacksmith. In 1890, his first son, Aron Szlama, came to the world, and on 22 February 1893, another, who was given the name Zishe. The couple finally married on 10 October 1894, when they already had two sons. Eventually there will be five more offspring. The children grew up in the spirit of Hasidism and used Yiddish. Like many families in this area they were very poor; none of its members could write or read.

The Breitbart family has been associated with Stryków from the mid-18th century. The genealogical tree of the future "King of Iron" shows the first inaccuracy in his traditional biography, which few people know. The original Zishe surname should be Brajtbart, not Breitbart. It appears as this on his official birth certificate. How was it changed? Was it a typical - often encountered, official mistake? It seems so. There are no other grounds that could explain why the name was changed. It appears to have happened just after the end of World War I when he began to be popular in Germany, perhaps to make it easier to pronounce. Throughout Zishe's life, his name appears in the form of Breitbart, but also Brajtbard, Brejtbard, Brajtbardt. It's the same with his first name. Depending on the country where he was staying, it was: Zysze, Zishe, Zisha, Zygmunt, Siegmund or Sigmund.

רבי אל׳ מנחם מ׳ זצ"ל
האדמו"ר מסטריקוב
עם בנו רבי יעקב יצחק דן
125   הי"ר

6. *Jewish men of Stryków*

His family was related to Levi Meir Brajtbart, a butcher who appears in the aforementioned memories of Stryków by Awroma Pinkas Unger entitled My town Stryków. This butcher was the brother of the future strongman's father. The maternal family came from Będzin, distant from Stryków, about 200 kilometers. At that point the cities were connected by rail.

In publications outside Poland, his place of birth is often referred to as "was born in 1893 in Starowieschtch (Starovitsch), Staro vietsch, Strikow, Strickau, Łódź - Strikow, in the city of Łódź, then part of imperial Russia". Stryków, and in fact its distorted name is considered an unspecified district of Lodz. You can also find the date of his birth given in the year 1883. Where did this date come from, the reader will learn a bit later, similarly to Łódź, also mentioned as a place of birth.

It has been told that around 1895-1896, little Zishe was almost crushed when a heavy metal grate in his father's forge fell on him. To the amazement of all he was able to free himself from the impediment, without much effort to remove the heavy object. From that moment, the parents closely watched the amazing strength of their little son. As he grew up Zishe continues to help his father when he worked in the forge.

7. In the Bible Samson fought the enemies of Israel

This event showed the unusual gift that Zishe Breitbart was endowed with for the first time, so began the story of a young Jewish boy who in the future will be proclaimed the Superman of the Ages. When he was a child in Stryków, there was another important event.

He was a very reflective child. One day he told his elder brother that in the future he wanted to be the "New Samson" who would fight the enemies of Israel. At the same time, he would ask the Rabbi at the synagogue in Stryków:

"Where are the Philistines, our greatest enemies"?

The rabbi apparently reacted to this question with a smile.

According to the Bible Samson is an example of God's calling of an individual man for the defense of the entire state. In Hebrew, "Samson" means sun or strong person, strongman. He was endowed with superhuman strength, which he used to fight Israel's enemies - the Philistines. He did acts impossible for ordinary people. The Philistines, in Hebrew, are alien, wandering people of Indo-European origin who, strove to control more and more of the areas as they expanded, falling into constant conflicts with the Israelites. The Israelites' oppression by the Philistines ended, according to the Bible, when Samson took up the fight with them.

In the pages of pre-war press publications in Poland, Jadwiga Rogozik wrote about him: "He dreamed of coming to Erec Israel as a modern Samson and doing heroic deeds that would draw the attention of the whole world to the creation of a Jewish state in Palestine."

At the time, he was asking about to the strongman Samson, for which his brother would tell him that such a person could only be in Eretz Israel[8]. Zishe had an unusual interest and curiosity to learn about the history of the Jewish people.

When he was five years old Zishe started learning in a cheder[9]. His mother wanted him to become a scholar. Meanwhile, starting at the age of eight, helped in the forge at the express request of his father. Finally, the father himself gave him the opportunity to choose between the two and he stayed in the forge.

As Zishe grew up, so did his strength. At the age of twelve or so, he started to practice something which would later be one of his own "numbers". Heavy stone slabs were laid on a trunk, which he broke with his hands. He would accomplish these feats without the slightest damage to himself.

---

8. The traditional Jewish name for an area of Israel
9. A traditional elementary school teaching the basics of Judaism and Hebrew

8. A silver Tetradrachma from Bar Kochba's time with the inscription "one year after the liberation of Israel"

The exhibition of his extraordinary strength was also supposed to be an event. Once, coming back from work in the forge, he spotted a pair of startled horses racing at him. They were harnessed to the wagon, chased by a woman with a man who were unable to stop them. Zishe was able to jump on the wagon and stop the crazed steeds.

He began to believe that the best place where he could present his unprecedented skills is the circus. Circuses visited Stryków every year. When was Zishe able to join the circus group for the first time? It is difficult to determine the exact date. In his publication *Zisha Breitbart (1893 - 1925) The Strongest Man in the World Jewish Defender*, Gary Bart, a relative of the strongman, informs us that he began his adventure with the circus for good at the age of fourteen. He started by fighting an unusual duel with ... circus bear.

This age was probable as boys between the ages of thirteen to fifteen often went to work during this era. It is also worth paying attention to the Bar Mitzvah celebrated by Jewish who have turned thirteen years old. On the first day after the thirteenth birthday they were considered an adult; already a man. From that day he was responsible to God for his actions and had to keep the commandments of the Mosaic Law. It is possible that it was after this feast that Zishe could leave the family home.

Around this time, he joined one of the circuses performing in Stryków. During the next few years, he performed in other traveling circuses, including Jewish ones. It was supposed to be a typically Gypsy life, and therefore he spent a lot of time traveling. This is how the first years of the future Superman of the Ages looked like.

Why, however, was it often said and commonly acknowledged that he was born in 1883?

The erroneous birth date of 1883 is related to the creation of his legend.

In 1887, the premiere of the operetta *Bar Kochba* took place, whose author was Abraham Goldfaden, a Jewish writer who is considered, among others, with the creator of a modern Jewish theater. This movement was connected in response to the pogroms of Jews that took place a few years earlier in 1883, mainly in the Moscow region of the Russian Empire. Like the titled hero from Roman times, it was hoped a man would rise to lead an army, which would free Jews from under oppression. Later, when Zishe Breitbart was already popular, the date of birth was moved just for the year of these pogroms. He was imagined as a contemporary of the Bar Kochba who was at the forefront of this uprising. That is why many saw the date of Zishe's birth in the year of these tragic events for the Jewish people. His birth date was used as a marketing idea to create an even greater legend - the long-awaited deliverer came into the world right after the huge persecutions of the entire nation took place.

The strongman repeatedly emphasized growing up that he was inspired by Samson and Bar Kochba. Ben Kutcher (Kuczer David Ber), in the strongman's biography published shortly after his death, mentions that his performances were modeled on the art of Bar Kokhba. The march, which was played when Zishe appeared on stage, was almost identical to the march from Goldfaden's performance. That's why he stylized himself as a warrior –a gladiator, which was supposed to be a reference to Roman times and the rise of Simon Bar Kokhba against the enslavement of Jews. In addition, the confirmation of this for many people writing about Zishe was the fact that by appearing in the circus as a teenager he was playing the role of the above-mentioned Jewish heroes. Hence, it explains the frequent use of Breitbart's birth in 1883.

Let's summarize again:

His performance strongly influenced some facts from Zishe's life, especially his date of birth. Even though the actual date of birth was placed on the tombstone was 1893, 1883 is often given as the date - the date of the pogroms in the Jewish community.

How do we explain this? He believed so strongly in his mission that the date of his birth was changed to one that would be more helpful in creating his legend!

20

9. The Jewish cemetery in Stryków, 1915

THE FIRST STRONGMEN - HEROES

Legends, histories and stories attribute extraordinary strength and amazing athletic performance to some people. Usually, they cannot be taken literally, because there are a lot of metaphors and generalizations in them. Some are also intended to show the spiritual properties of the nation, reflected in the heroic feats of favorite heroes. These heroes are above all seen as great patriots defending their homeland, and their deeds are mainly military successes. They fight against hostile enemies, as well as evil people and monsters, and they build upon many other great deeds to the glory of their native land. These actions are characterized by nobility and selflessness. Such strongmen fight for the safety of honest people. Not all old legends are fantastic, often there is some truth in them. Sometimes you can find real historical roots of some of the legendary heroes and strongmen.

The ancient Greek athlete Milonie of Croton, who was the seven-time winner at the Olympic Games, once supposedly circled the arena four times carrying a four-year-old bull on his shoulders. On the stone in Olympia, an inscription was engraved: "Bybon, son of Phola, lifted me with one hand over his head." That stone weighed 143 kilograms. We also all know the mythical Hercules, who was considered a demigod because of his superhuman strength. As an infant, he strangled snakes, when he was a child he killed lions, in his youth he crushed rocks, and as a mature husband he took on the weight of the entire sky. In Jewish culture, Samson was the equivalent of the invincible hero struggling for freedom.

At the beginning of the twentieth century, regular visitors to circuses - experiencing their boom at that time - could once again enjoy a rare spectacle. The main attraction was the event when a huge lion was released into the arena with a muzzle and leather gloves glued to the paws. Then a man came out, wearing only sports shorts. After a few minutes of fighting, the athlete would hold the lion over his head, weighing more than a quarter of a ton. Feats of strength by strongmen were admired everywhere they appeared. Towards the end of the

19th century, the athlete Rollen Bezzębny wandered through the cities and villages of France and Belgium. At one of the street performances, Rollen put four 20-kilo weights, an iron axle weighing 73 kg, on his horse and then put his wife on the saddle. Then he tied the horse's front and back legs, went under the animal's belly, and he carried the weight of about 470 kilos over his shoulders. With this enormous weight he circled the parade ground twice. Another strong man, the French peasant, Karol Roucelle, who later became a professional athlete, lifted a table with a weight weighing a ton, and thus exceeding 17 times its weight. These amazing records were established without applying any rules to the sport. Therefore, it is not always possible to vouch for the accuracy of the weight. It is also difficult to compare the results and decide which of these athletes was stronger, because these results were achieved in completely different conditions.

10. Abe Attell

At the beginning of the twentieth century, there were also Jewish heroes of world renown. It should be emphasized that most of them originated from Poland and they were Polish Jews.

Before World War I, Avram Vildman was a famous wrestler in Warsaw. Reading the press from that period, we find a report that when he loses a bout, he does not leave the mat, the Jews in the audience start singing psalms to cheer him up. Boxers were also very popular. Abe Attell was called the "Little Jew," to whom, among other things, this term and problems with the law made it impossible to sign himself up for important matches was a Jewish hero. The same was with Ruby Goldstein, who was victorious, but not in the most important boxing

11. Abi Coleman

matches. It was not until Benny Leonard, the boxer with his greatest successes coming in the years 1917 - 1925, received a flattering comparison - it was said that he is more known than Albert Einstein. In the years 1923 - 1924 when Breitbart became a sensation with his performances in America, he had emigrated to there from Poland, the Jewish wrestler Abi Coleman (actually Abe Kelmer) from Zychlin. He fought among others in New York's Madison Square Garden. He was one of the few Jewish wrestlers of this time, given the nickname "Jewish Tarzan" and "Hebrew Hercules". He later died at the age of 101. These terms referred to the superhuman strength that he showed. In 1893, also in Suwałki, Poland, Joseph Greenstein, later a strongman, came into the world. Despite its small height and weight of around 63 kilograms, he became one of the top strongmen of the 20th century. His exploits were somewhat reminiscent of Breitbart's skill. Like him, he could, for example, simultaneously break three chains, bend iron rods and horseshoes or lay on a bed made of nails. He also began his career in a traveling circus.

Despite the huge popularity among the Jewish population, none of them achieved the popularity of Zishe. They were hindered, inter alia, by some insinuations related to their personal life. Breitbart as one of the few had to combine strength with the intellect.

12. Benny Leonard

BREITBART'S STRENGTH

Everyone seems to have some talent for their lives. In ancient times they developed a whole training set to develop their talents which they put in two words: beauty and strength. It is believed that anyone who wanted to manage their own development must know the properties of their bodies - individually and those that are common to all people. It is assumed that the period of proper maturation occurs in boys from 14 to 18 years of age. During Breitbart's popularity, it was believed that strength training must not be started before the age of 21. It was only in the first years after the end of World War II that this view radically changed. In the US, strength training was introduced as a trial for boys aged 12-14 years. Some began to achieve sensational results, but generally it did not apply just for athletes. People strove to develop the strong muscles, but those who tried to exercise with too much too early were often seriously hurt. Strength exercises that started around 14 - 15 years of age were preceded by dexterity exercises. Speed, agility and strength are three important features of physical fitness, the first two of which are easiest to acquire in their youth. One must also strive to pliable and flexible, to move freely in exhibition. It is recommended to use various forms of gymnastics, which are best done briskly - in a trot. Nutrition is also extremely important. Strength training based on the one's own body weight was already known in ancient times. It consisted of performing six exercises to help strengthen and sculpt all parts of the body (pull-ups, push-ups, squats, lifting legs, push-ups on the handrails and exercises of the bridge strengthening the spine muscles). The diet of old gladiators was often vegetarian, where they were often eating legumes. It was supplemented with drinks with a lot of calcium. Because of this they are often called "barley eaters". By the time Breitbart became popular, the absence of meat was pointed out to him as a huge mistake.

BREITBART MUSCLE GUIDE

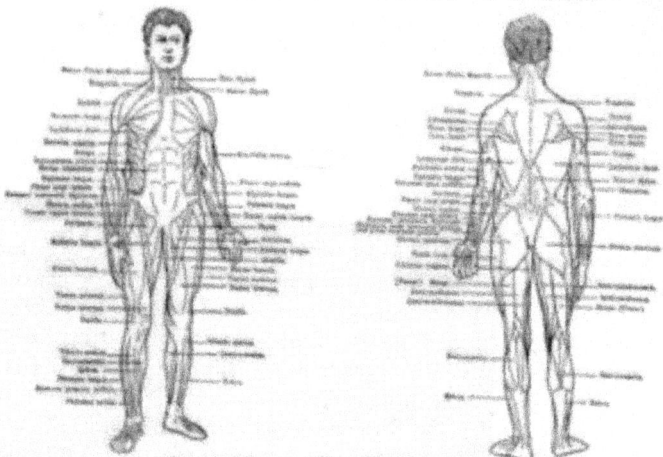

13. A section from Breitbart's book, Muscular Strength

WHO AND WHY DID ZISHE OWE HIS STRENGTH?

According to the division of body types drawn up by Ernest Kretschmer, a doctor and psychiatrist, who talked about the characteristic features of the human body structure, Zishe belonged to what he labeled "athletic type". It is characterized by a regular body structure with a strongly developed muscular and bony system with a short skull, a hairline equal to the forehead and a square face. From a medical point of view, such people may have a tendency toward cardiovascular disease - which was confirmed in Breitbart's case. Did he inherit the constitution of his body, or a set of anatomical and physiological conditions of his organs were genetic? Probably yes, because two of his brothers were also distinguished by exceptional strength and his sister was also considered a strong woman. In addition, his grandfather and father were also supposed to be an exceptional strong which was useful in their profession. It should be remembered that some exercises require extraordinary strength to perform, which necessitates knowing what your abilities are. But also, as Breitbart's great idol Harry Houdini explained, for example, many metal locks, handcuffs can be opened in a simple way using even ... a shoelace. Strength must go hand in hand with intelligence.

Zishe was 185 centimeters tall[10], weighing 102 kilograms[11]. The circumference of the chest was 127 centimeters[12], and his waist was 90 centimeters[13] in circumference. He did not have the construction of a typical muscular athlete, but he emphasized the beautiful and muscular proportional of his body (it was written that he was shaped like Adonis, handsome as Valentino, slim as a leopard). He also exhibited good manners in everyday life with intelligent humor. In turn, *Leipziger Neueste Nachrichten* recalls his performance in Leipzig in 1920, where he played with the Schumann Circus at Albert Hall. The performance was

---

10. 6'2"
11. 224 lbs
12. 50"
13. 35.4"

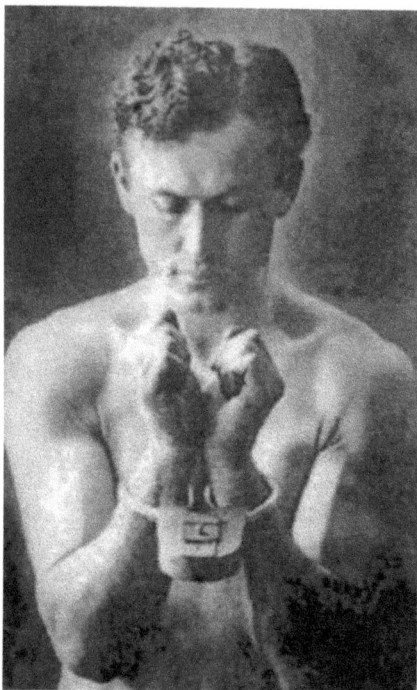

14. Harry Houdini, the great illusionist, was one of Breitbart's idols

a great triumph, which they felt was astonishing because he did not look like a great muscular strongman. Examples of Karl Rappo, Karl Abso, Emil Raucke and the Rasso brothers are given.

In an interview with the Viennese newspaper *Volks - Zeitung* on 30 November 1922, Zishe remembered his father, who at the age of 65 worked as a blacksmith with the enthusiasm and energy of a young man. He also mentions one of his brothers who died during World War I. The newspaper, however, does not avoid mistakes, saying that Zishe is thirty-one years old at the time. At that time in Vienna, a medical conference took place, which dealt with examining the amazing feats of the strongman. It was decided that unknown anomalies of his body were behind his extraordinary abilities. The interview also included Artur Georgis, who was a friend of a strongman and at the same time a manager organizing the majority of his foreign trips.

For the science of the time he remained, a miracle of nature. Other Jewish leaders from Central and Eastern Europe claimed that he was pursuing the Semitic ideal of beauty. He was the embodiment of gentleness and modesty. This was also considered the ideal of the physique of the Jewish manhood in this part of Europe.

And here is the way to maintain physical fitness according to Breitbart and favorite life lesson sayings. This fragment comes from the collection of Gary Bart.

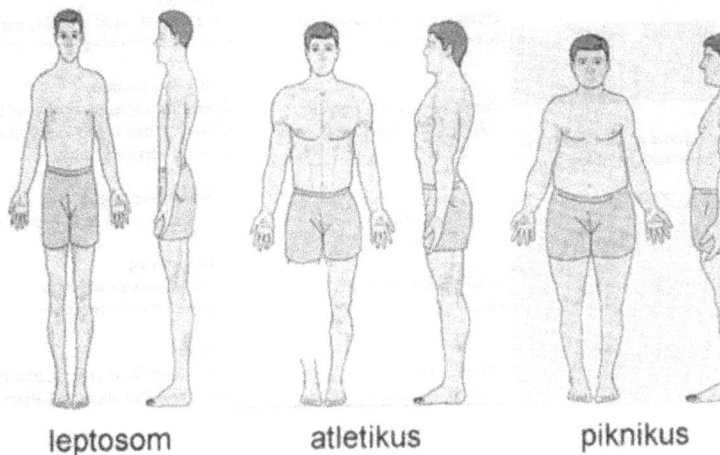

leptosom   atletikus   piknikus

15. Body types based on the divisions of Ernest Kretschmer – willowy, athletic, heavy

A DAY IN BREITBART'S LIFE

Breitbart got up very early. Right after dressing he started training his body. He began with Swedish gymnastics and then step by step to more complex routines using a machine he developed himself. After exercising he took a brief rest and then went for a walk or drive.

At 12:00 noon he has tea.
At 1:00 p.m.an extensive breakfast
Between 2:00 and 3:00 he receives visitors
Between 3:00 and 5:00 he trains or engages in sports
At 6:00 p.m. Supper: lots of soup, pasta, vegetables, fruit and fish.

After supper he eats nothing else and an hour before bedtime he drinks a glass of milk.

Thus, Breitbart (1) ate very little meat; (2) led a very regulated life; (3) does not drink alcoholic beverages – except for an occasional glass of wine or beer; (4) does not soak in a tub; (5) Makes time for himself, goes on car excursions, mostly driving himself. In addition, he engages in sports: horseback riding, rowing, flying, tennis etc.

CONSCRIPTION TO THE ARMY, THE BEGINNING OF A GREAT CAREER

In 1914 Zishe was 20 years old. In accordance with the Russian law then in force in the Kingdom of Poland, he was available for conscription, and therefore available for military service. That's how it happened, for so many years. In that year there were two classes of conscripts, spring and autumn. Military service lasted five or six years depending on the branch of the military. The class of 1893 was ordered to present themselves. This forced him to stop his adventures with the circus. As it soon turned out, it was a conscription in the year of the outbreak of the Great World War. We will never know what the future "Iron King" would have fared if he got into the army earlier, instead of the years of the Great World War. No one in Europe thought that the outbreak of war would have such a revolutionary influence on the continent's fate. Zishe himself did not suppose that conscription, military service and wartime experiences would change his life. The mobilization and conscription into the army took place in the last days of July and the beginning of August. A year before being recruited, his mother Zelda Gitla died. The Breitbart family was still among the poor of Stryków.

In the Kingdom of Poland (recall - this was the name of the Polish lands included in the Russian partition), which included Stryków, lived 1.3 million Jews, (about fourteen percent of the total population). Zishe was one of 350,000 Jewish soldiers mobilized to the Tsarist army. On 1 August 1914, the Germans declared war on Russia. The Tsarist army was focused on an offensive towards Berlin. In November and December, Łódź and its surroundings became the center of attention in the global conflict. It was here in Zishe's homeland that the fate of the war was to be resolved: the Russians planned to move towards Berlin, and the Germans planned to circle around the enemy. It quickly turned out that the situation of the Tsarist army was not good. In mid-December, the commander-in-chief of the Russian army, Grand Duke Nikolaj Nikolayevich, issued a statement

16. The German Army requisitions supplies in Stryków

saying that "circumstances forced the order to suspend offensive operations". Both armies became stuck in the trenches.

Where did Zishe fight, on which campaigns at the front?

This time in his life contains the several questions. We have several different similar stories, but they were placed different time periods.

According to one of them, he was serving in the artillery, fighting in "Western Russia" and became a prisoner of war in East Prussia in 1916 (where there were camps for Russian prisoners of war). These battles took place in Poland, in the region of Masuria. He remained in captivity until the end of the war and at that time he honed his skills to charm both Russians and Germans. When the war ended, Zishe decided to stay in Germany.

He kept up giving shows on fairs, streets, squares, which in those days for people remembering the nightmare of the recently completed war was great entertainment diversion. It was thanks to such shows that local idols were created,

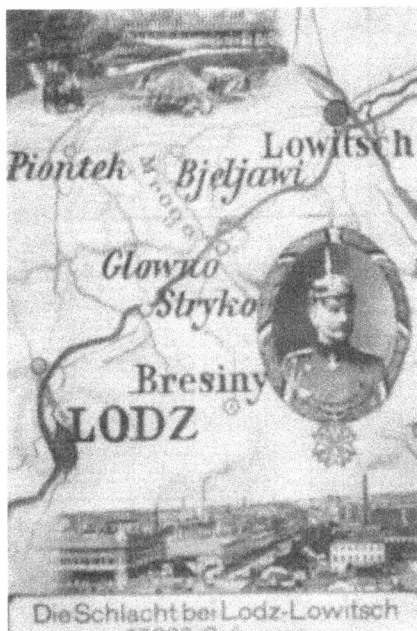

17. A German postcard depicting the successes of this army during WWI in central Poland which shows Stryków

which were later told about as legends. The representatives of the largest circuses reached out and watched such people. Stories of a strongman who could do inexplicable and impossible things for a normal man reached the director of one of the most famous European circus owned by Paul Busch - called Circus Busch (now Circus Busch-Roland). He had personally watched several exhibitions by Zishe in Bremen and Hamburg. He did not think long about hiring the strongman which took place in 1919 and from then Breitbart's popularity grew daily. At the same time, he married Emilie Ester Weitz, daughter of a German rabbi.

According to yet another story he served, as previously stated, in the artillery. He was taken prisoner after he was serving in an artillery unit despite the death of the soldiers around him. While staying in captivity, he continued to make sure he boxed and continued physical training. When he regained his freedom, he was sent to Moscow along with the first evacuation group of soldiers in captivity. Two extraordinary stories arise out of this tale. The first is he saved a woman from jumping from a window who wanted to commit suicide. He caught her in his arms on the run, thereby saving her life. In the second relates that he rescued a one-and-a-half-year-old child from a burning apartment on the third floor. The fire-ladder ladder could not reach that high, so he threw a piece of rope over the window frame and thus got inside the room. Then, on the same line, he lowered the child in the cradle to the ground, while he himself jumped from the burning window on the fireman's ladder and without any obstacles went down the steps.

There is also the third version, which is told by Gary Bart. This was very similar to the second version, but the difference is that he saved a woman and a child

35

that could have occurred somewhere in Russia at the beginning of the war. Was it Moscow? The author does not write anything about it. However, he gives information that it was Polish Countess, whom he calls Tatyana, that was saved. What we know for sure is that the strongman was indeed been taken prisoner during operations at the front. At that time, he was also supposedly working as a prisoner in a factory in Germany. At that time, he was met the great love, his future wife, for whom he had to go to Cologne in secret on board the ship.

Gary Bart says that when the war ended, our hero returned to an independent Poland. The countess who he saved paid for his trip to America. He was supposed to go to New York where he learned professional strength training and wrestling. However, it was known that he would return to Europe soon to get married and start performing in small circuses. His fame and exploits began to grow, and he received more and more offers until finally Bremen where he delighted with the head of the most popular circus in Europe, Paul Busch. So, he began appearances in Circus Busch in 1919.

18. Erik Jan Hanussen conducting a seance

The second and third version of the strongman's fortune also tells what happened next. Once again, they are very similar, but located in a different time, stories. Around the beginning of 1919, according to the accounts of one of the Polish newspapers described in 1925, he was supposed to go to ... New York. The trip was possible thanks to the financial help of the woman whose life saved his life. In the beginning it was difficult because he did not know the language and could not get any job. Then, he was supposedly a hit with the audience of one of the local circuses. In one circus an athlete came out on stage bending metal bars, he supposedly made an offer to the audience declaring that he would offer $100 to anyone who could beat him in wrestling. Breitbart dared and beat the wrestler, so his great career began.

It was during this stay that he also became acquainted with the clairvoyant Erik Jan Hanussen and his partner, Marta Farra, in *The New York Times* for the first time. This woman's unusual act consisted in lifting an adult elephant. It turned out, however, that a concealed chain was dropped, which helped the entertainer to lift the burden. One of the guests saw this and started a riot. Farra was almost lynched by the American crowd. Breitbart saved her, and when he went into the arena he suggested to the audience that he would repeat her number. Putting

19. Zishe Breitbart during a circus performance

the chain around the elephant's neck, he raised his head up and the elephant hung in the air. The newspaper further reported that "this incident put Breitbart on the road to fame. "Is this story reliable? It seems not, and it was created as a combination and compilation of various facts from the life of the strongman written after his death.

Soon after performances in Berlin, Dresden, Leipzig, Hamburg or Wroclaw, the Breitbart name became a synonymous for strength and power. Mothers would say to their children: eat and be strong like Breitbart. That's how the world-class strongman's career began. He again permanently returned to the town he was born and raised. After his performances in Germany, he was called a "Jewish" strongman.

A special artistic program was prepared for him, which referred to the young "blacksmith's" life. The most popular feats that the audience cared were:

- placing a special platform on his chest, upon which was placed two motorcycles.

- the passage of a car filled with people lying while Breitbart was on his back, the same number was also repeated on his chest.

- breaking metal chains and biting them –which was so easy that it looked like biting cookies, chewing coins.

- breaking horseshoes, bending metal rods, mostly in floral patterns, he often did it by holding a metal rod in his teeth.

- on his head a long piece of iron was laid, on which a dozen or so men hung themselves from each side and in this way, it bent him.

- pulling wagons, locomotives, horse and mechanical vehicles with a chain in his teeth.

- lifting a small elephant while climbing the ladder, while holding a wheel from a locomotive in his teeth, to which three men were suspended.

- a number called the Tomb of Hercules consisting of a bridge built on his torso, after which the elephants were paraded, the same number was made with the setting of concrete blocks on the chest.

- breaking stone plates on his chest with hammers.

- in the Staniewski Circus in Poland, there was a special number in which Breitbart held a motordrome on his chest - a silo similar a huge barrel, inside of which two motorcyclists rode.

20. Another example of Zishe Brietbart's circus performance

- keeping two horses in the hands of the harness, which although they tried to go, they could not move.

- nailing with bare hands

In 1920, he was already referred to as the strongest man on Earth - the Jewish Superman. In addition to the phenomenal power of the spectacular nature of his performances, he was also distinguished by his acting talent. All this combined with intelligence built his myth, his personality. He gathered a library of about 2,000 items about the history of ancient Rome

He had a gentle, delicate personality, and was often compared to the film idol of that time Rudolf Valentino. He admitted in one of the interviews that when taking a walk, he makes sure that he does not step on worms. He liked small animals. To him, manhood consisted of strength, but also of delicacy. That is why he was also referred to as the "Polish Apollo". Though this was in jest, these were the skills that he demonstrated, wanting to draw attention to the situation of the Jewish community.

Over the next two years, shows in the most important European cities make him a wealthy man. He finally settled on the outskirts of Berlin. And that's where unique events take place! Breitbart's Villa - that's what his residence was called - was always an open house for the poor and for people in need of help. They could always count on his support. Photographs showed queues of people in front of the house are waiting for help.

Isn't this event consistent with the personality of the comic Superman? He gave selfless help to the disadvantaged! He did it even though no one demanded it from him! This thing is basically unheard of in such a commercialized world!

He married Emilie Ester Weitz (born 1889) in 1919. She was the daughter of Rabbi Dr. Weitz from Koblenz. They raised a son named Ossi, who was born in 1920.

His idols were at that time the Jewish boxer, lightweight champion Benny Leonard and Harry Houdini one of the most famous illusionists, specializing in aerobatics, as well as the debunker of the spiritualist media. He was able to free himself from chains, even when he was suspended on a rope and was under water. He performed in the USA and he was extremely popular there before Zishe conquered their hearts.

In 1922 he was a guest of the Jewish Congress in Leipzig. At that time, the Nazis under NSDAP were growing in Germany. It is just such a group of nearly 200 people who attacked the meeting. Zishe broke into the ranks of Nazi militants and attacked, trying to chase the demonstrators. From that time, it was recommended to him to maintain a security detail when giving public performances.

One of his numbers, which will be extremely popular in America in a few years first occurred in Warsaw. This was happening in Aleja Szucha where he managed to stop a platform harnessed by a pair of horses. The crowds hurrying to watch the strong man were so large and so interested in the event that it was difficult for several hours to get through Ujazdowskie Street. Yes, so one of the most important streets in Warsaw was blocked. This performance was done to support a charitable organization helping the poor.

Blick v. Villa Breitbart zum Dorf Friedrichsthal.

Allee zur Kirche.

21. Villa Breitbart on the outskirts of Berlin where Zishe used to live

41

VIENNA, THE BIRTH OF
A LEGEND AND A DISPUTE
WITH FUTURE FRIEND
OF NAZI STRONGMAN

By the end of December 1922 Zishe found himself in Vienna, where his performances lasted for over three months! We know their description thanks to a publication by Professor Sharon Gillerman focusing on Jewish history entitled, *Samson in Vienna*.[14]

At that time, Vienna was a city in which anti-Semitic sentiments grew, and Jewish self-defense was organized to defend against the hate groups. He was greeted as a hero upon his arrival where he was announced as the "New Samson." As he left the railway carriage, he was greeted by a special stylized car modeled on a chariot, drawn by two white horses. Seeing this, he threw off his cloak, appearing in a Roman gladiator's outfit covered with a white-blue cloak with the star of David on it. A special metal buckle was fastened to the horse harness, which Zishe took to his lips and pulled a car carrying forty passengers. This manner of greeting the audience was inevitably repeated by him during each performance. He became a phenomenon, the idol of Vienna, about which much was written in the press, and at the mention of his name "the image of other professional athletes was forgotten".

The outfit of a Roman gladiator or a warrior of Roman legions he wore was a reference to the former Jewish hero Bar - Kochba, mentioned earlier. He was the commander of the Jewish uprising against Rome in the years 132 - 135 of our era. As a result of these victories, Bar-Kochba, he ruled an independent Jewish state for a short period. It was re-conquered by Romans after two years and he

---

14. Sharon Gillerman, "Samson in Vienna: The Theaters of Jewish Masculinity," *Jewish Social Studies* 9:2 (Winter, 2003), p. 65.

22. Zishe appeared in the Roman gladiator's dress and wore a cape

was killed. Jerusalem was ultimately erased from the face of the earth, and the few survivors were forced to go into miserable exile, without the right to return to their hometown. This leader of the uprising really was called Ber Kosiba, his name was changed to Bar Kochba, and in Aramaic it meant "Son Stars "and referred to the Book of Numbers in which the rising Star of Jacob is spoken off. Zishe played his role; he took up the role of Jewish hero, this time associated with the biblical hero - Samson, who takes up the struggle for the independence of his nation as the "New Samson". These performances sought to legitimize the Jewish rights to autonomy, which he especially articulated in countries strongly associated with Christianity. He wanted to symbolize the "body" of the Jewish people. In addition, he was proclaimed a philanthropist, because it happened that he often gave money to the needy.

The circus performances were an opportunity for Breitbart to be a Zionist, a space of a political manifesto. He exhibited his involvement in this movement by placing an announcement on the posters calling his performances of the new Samson including the star of David. These spectacles displayed the strength of the muscles in reference to the idea of muscular Judaism, which created a controversial image to show the Jewish people of the Bible. In sporting exercises, while Breitbart wanted to be seen as the expression of the nation's activity, he was dismissed by some people as a tool for integration of Jewish people into everyday life. He believed that through the development of the body, as a symbolic image, it became the formula for the invention of the national community. Therefore, the most important inspiration for him was ancient Rome. Because of his fascination, he collected books and materials on the subject. This also explains why he was the only German centurion in Germany. He wanted to give a new meaning to this old Roman spectacle. This was happening when the German fondness for the Rome of that era, was widely regarded as the unsurpassed pattern of power and military perfection, that was ever known. Zishe played in the Roman circuses as a Roman centurion. But, he was presented as a Germanic warrior in Roman armor when he entered the stage there with Wagner's music from Siegfried's opera playing in the background.

During his performance in Vienna he met with the extremely influential financier and banker, Ludwig Rothschild, who invited him to tea. Zishe accepted the invitation, and the meeting was also attended by influential and wealthy and Viennese. Rothschild asked him to show off his strength. In response, the strongman lifted the piano with one hand and a huge table with the other. The host supposedly joked about it by saying:

You raise everything up, you cannot raise our currency". He was supposed heard the answer:

"To raise the currency, Mr. Rothschild, you need your action, not mine."

Guests liked the Breitbart joke. It was at a time when the Austrian currency was rapidly depreciating as a result of inflation. During this time, he was swamped with fan mail. The hotel where he lived was so inundated that he published a request in the pages of all the newspapers in Vienna, that they should stop writing and visiting him because he did not even have time to eat. The management of the Vienna Post reported that no citizen had ever received such a large number of letters a day. They were mostly sent by people asking him for support.

Of course, there were those who did not believe his skills. One of them was the aforementioned Erik Jan Hanussen, whose actually name was Harry Steinschneider, who hid his Jewish origins, and who claimed to be an aristocrat from Denmark. His main irritation was the popularity Zishe enjoyed in Vienna and the fight for the primacy of recognition among the Jewish community. Hanussen and his paranormal abilities based on occult visions and prophecies made him as special as Zishe. He appeared in cabarets and theaters at the same time as Zishe, as a magician with certain telepathic abilities. He sought to undermine belief in the strength of Zishe, claiming that he could create a person of similar and even greater strength than Breitbart by means of various parapsychological tricks.

Performing in Vienna he came in conflict with Hanussen, a feud that lasted for many years and was later immortalized on film. It all began with the performance of the strongman on the stage of the prestigious "Ronacher" theater in Vienna. Hanussen claimed that Breitbart got the show thanks to its director, Rosner, who served as captain of the cavalry during the First World War in the Austro-Hungarian army. Hanussen proposed Zishe perform with him in a different theater. He received a refusal as a reply. Hanussen then began a media campaign to denigrate Breitbart. For example, he funneled information to the press that the strongman had confessed to him that all steel and iron products that he breaks, and bends were ordered from his blacksmith. The blacksmith, in turn, producing them to leave hallow interiors and therefore allowing them to be broken with great ease. The audience who were supposedly delighted after seeing all these shows were then bribed with a share of the income raised to speak highly of him. Hanussen constantly called on Breitbart to show his real strength in another theater and use the instruments he prepared himself. The strongman did not respond to these remarks. At the same time, his secretary, Aga Dzino, followed Breitbart and reported every detail of his private life. The slanderer, seeing that his efforts did not bring the desired effects, came up with another idea. He began to publicize and advertise the abilities of extraordinary young girl Marta Fara (Marta Kohn - Martha Cohen, also known as Martha Farra). As her impresario, he wrote about her: "The greatest miracle of nature from the twentieth century! Miss Marta Fara breaks the chains like buns, bends iron like straw, surpasses Breitbart by her strength. " Hanussen managed to cause confusion because the audience was divided into "Breitbartists" and "Pharaists". Both groups had their supporters and opponents. Every day in the theater where they appeared there were scandals from both sides of supporters. In the end it turned out that Marta Fara was a cheat and the objects which she used to demonstrate her strength were not real and counterfeit.

23. An Austrian newspaper describing Breitbart's trial against Hanussen

Hanussen, however, did not give up and on 4 February 1923 in the pages of one of the Viennese newspapers *Der Tag* he accused Breitbart of fraud and called for a public duel between him and Martha Kohn (Martha Farra). He declared that he would donate huge amounts of money to charity if Breitbart was able to break the iron chains he had supplied him and if his "Queen Marta Farra" was not be able to repeat the same of the strongman's exploits. He also promised that he would find twenty more strongmen who could demonstrate similar skills as Zishe, concerning bending steel bars.

Breitbart downplayed Hanussen's boasts, most likely because the movie *"King of Iron"* depicting his skills was shot at that time. It was a great event that would further strengthen his image, and director Max Neufeld took up the challenge. Finally, Breitbart filed a lawsuit against the slanders of Hanussen, and both of them met in the Vienna court. The result of the dispute was unusual, probably surprising both sides: Breitbart was charged a high fine, and Hanussen had to leave Austria for some time. This event will be recalled in a slightly different context several dozen years later with the help of the film *"Invincible"* by Werner Herzog. Soon, performances in Vienna or Prague among the Jewish communities allowed him to collect the equivalent of the fine. His fans even invented a special parody played on the stage telling about Breitbart's competition against Hanussen which enjoyed great popularity for some time.

While Hanussen was expelled from Austria, Breitbart's myth continued to grow. Because of this Zishe had to hide his whereabouts to get some peace. For example, when it was discovered which restaurant he would eat lunch, he was immediately besieged by crowds of people. His popularity grew further because fans appreciated his free performances to philanthropic institutions that brought them huge profits.

Many newspapers with different political and social beliefs still praised his deeds. They proclaimed it was very important to emphasize watching his performances, saying that "Judah's strain has not expired". This meant that as long as Breitbart and his inexplicable abilities existed, there would be Jewish culture.

24. Strongman demonstrates his favorite number-bending metal rods in floral patterns

He appeared everywhere and demonstrated his skills to many people, but raised the question: Is this inhuman power? It was also written that "no one is able to understand this miracle of nature." Of course, he aroused great interest even among professors of medicine who want to know the phenomenon of his skills. He was examined in various ways and each time a statement was issued that the body building and strength of muscles does not exceed many other strongmen. Where did this unusual strength come from? No one could answer such a question.

Behind the words were also deeds. Zishe was a guest at

many restaurants. But he ceased to attend some of them when the orchestras entertaining the audience in them, refused to play "Hatikvah" - the hymn of Israel "Hope" at his request. This played into his dream of leading an army, which would return to Erec Israel (The Land of Israel).

Erec Israel - the Land of Israel is the land promised to the God-Chosen People, whom the Jews intended to revive. One of the main representatives of the Zionist movement, Teodor Herzl, claimed that the Jews were in Israel. For some, settling in the land of ancestors was an expression of the religious conviction that Erec Israel is a more perfect country than other countries in the world, and Jerusalem is a more perfect city than other cities. For the second time, the return to Israel was an expression of the desire to create a modern state, the realization of dreams that could not be fulfilled where Jews had lived for centuries. In November 1918, Palestine was divided into a Jewish and Arabic part. These territories transformed into Israel and Arab Palestine.

After the performances in Vienna, he was no longer just a circus performer or a vaudeville artist. His character was surrounded by the aura of mysticism, and at times viewed as almost divine. He is credited with superhuman abilities, deeds and a mission he had to fulfill.

This event is also important because it began to emphasize not only its physical strength. "If there were thousands of Brietbart's between Jews in the world, then there would never have been persecutions" - that is how the dream of the Jewish community aroused from this moment is determined in a short order.

During his performances in Vienna in 1922, he was again examined by some of the most eminent doctors of the city who declared that the body building and the strength of his muscles was not exceed by many other strongmen. "No human brain is able to penetrate this miracle of nature. This argument still raises his strength in our eyes and allows us without hesitation to call him the new Samson."

In 1923, Zishe also hit the cinema screens. His skills were admired in the aforementioned film directed by Max Neufeld entitled *Der Eisenkönig* or *The Iron King*, but that was not all. It was also possible to see him in the film *Schmalbart als KANN`UTZEN*. Wytwórnia Stadt Film Wien made a 28-minute, silent movie entitled *Wo sich das?* (*Where is That?*) telling about life in Vienna where in one of his sequences Zishe bends a metal rod holding it in his teeth. His image began to be used in advertisements and even on Christmas cards.

25. A poster from the film "King of Iron" about Zishe Breitbart's life

SUPERMAN OF NEW YORK AND SUPERMAN OF THE AGES

The time had come to conquer America. If it is possible to gain fame there, it is usually immortal. In the summer of 1923, Zishe was officially invited to a series of performances in the United States and Canada. He convinced the naysayers and was finally able to solidify his reputation with his uncommon skills. He found himself on the American soil on 26 August 1923. What happened exceeded all expectations. The press proclaimed, "Jewish Superman" had come to Manhattan, while *The New York Times* called him "the phenomenon of the ages". An atmosphere of mystery and interest was promoted and built around it. Newspapers such as the *New York Telegraph*, *The Brooklyn Times*, and *The New*

26. Breitbart has been called Superman since the 1920s

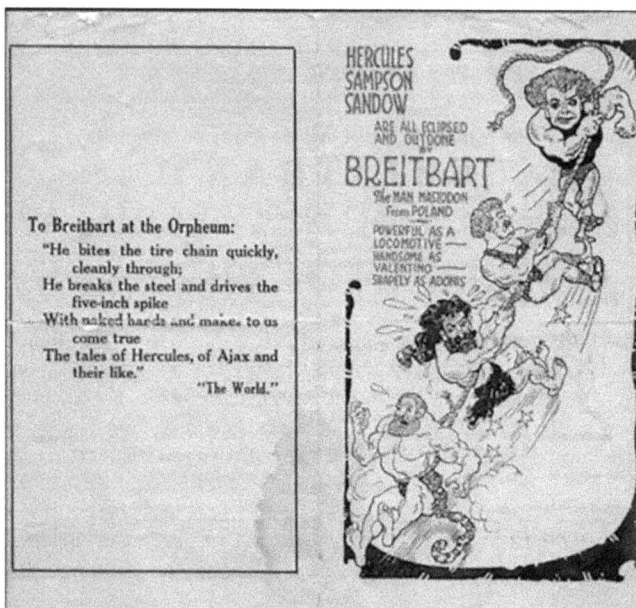

To Breitbart at the Orpheum:

"He bites the tire chain quickly, cleanly through;
He breaks the steel and drives the five-inch spike
With naked hands and makes to us come true
The tales of Hercules, of Ajax and their like."

"The World."

HERCULES
SAMPSON
SANDOW
ARE ALL ECLIPSED
AND OUTDONE
BY
BREITBART
The MAN MASTODON
From POLAND
POWERFUL AS A
LOCOMOTIVE —
HANDSOME AS
VALENTINO —
SHAPELY AS ADONIS

27. A program from one of Breitbart's performances

York Star ran special columns devoted to Zishe Breitbart and his performances. He was called "a superman in physical fitness and perfection". It turned out that it was worth promoting. Newspapers that devote special spots to his shows even wrote that Breitbart's performances were one of the most important events in American history!

After the performance on 8 September 1923, the critics in the Orpheum Theater in Brooklyn wrote that he beat all previous attendance records. Five days later, *The New York Evening* announced with pride that "the best man for electrifying audiences in the world has applied for US citizenship and will soon be our countryman." No wonder he was granted American citizenship.

Zishe's fame and legend in America grew day by day. In the fall of 1923, he was a star in such cities as Providence, Buffalo, Toronto, Cleveland, Chicago, Pittsburgh, Baltimore, and Washington. In Washington on 27 November 1923, one of the most popular and well-known photograph of Zishe was taken in Washington. Surrounded by a few men, he's holding a chain in his teeth attached to a wagon, on one of Washington's streets during the attempt to set a record. Zishe dragged the wagon with fifty people in it.

In New York during the Christmas period, he performed at the Hippodrome, playing before eighty-five thousand spectators over that period, breaking all previous records. His weekly *receipts* were $ 7,000, ($102,000 in 2018 dollars) which was an exorbitant amount you could only dream of during that time.

From that time forward, we have very interesting posters or programs (folders) promoting people to watch his performances. This is where we have the first inferences that there is Superman who can stop a speeding locomotive. Some of these references can be seen later in the Superman comic book!

During performances in New York and Chicago, a rumor spread by the wealthy entrepreneur Henry Ford (who was a known anti-Semitic) questioning Zishe's skills. The strong man offered Ford to prove that using the shackles chosen by his accuser he could free himself within fifteen minutes. If he won, Ford would lose this plant, and he would give half of his assets to Erec Israel. The industrialist did not accept the proposal, and the proud Breitbart himself donated a huge sum of money for this purpose. In view of the huge audience, he made his point. From that time on, critics would stop all attacks on his person.

28. A broadsheet for one of Zishe's performances which show some of Superman's characteristics

An Unequalled Bill of Vaudeville Celebrities!

WEEK OF MARCH 3RD, 1924

—Beginning with Monday Matinee—

SPECIAL RETURN ENGAGEMENT!

ARTHUR GEORGIS Presents   The Sensation of Two Continents

SIEGMUND BREITBART

The Iron King

Direct from His New York Hippodrome Engagement of Eight Weeks, Where Capacity Audiences
Marvelled at His Marvelous Strength
During His Engagement Here He Will Exhibit New and Original Strength Feats

GEO. WATTS & BELLE HAWLEY	AL—MARKELL & GAY—NELL
In Laughs Coated With Melodies	Dancers Par Excellence

A New One-Act Comedy

"A FRIEND IN NEED, ETC."

With MANN HOLINER & NICHOLAS JOY
A Case of Mistaken Identity With a New Angle, by HOWARD EMMETT ROGERS

Vaudeville's Newest Musical Classic

MARIE DAWSON MORRELL

America's Own Violinist and Phonograph Artist
ROYAL BERNARD at the Piano

KAY & LORENE STERLING	LES GHEZZI
Present a Sterling Offering	Equilibrists, Strong and Courageous

AESOP'S FABLES	TOPICS OF THE DAY	PATHE NEWS

EXTRA ADDED ATTRACTION!	AND	EXTRA ADDED ATTRACTION

Vaudeville's Latest Comedy Sensation!

MISS RAY DOOLEY *and*
MR. FLORENZ AMES

In "A TERPSICHOREAN DILEMMA"
By JOSEPH CAWTHORNE, Assisted by EBEN S. LITCHFIELD

TWO SHOWS DAILY: 2 and 8 P. M. PRICES: Matinees, 30c, 55c and 85c. NIGHTS: 50c to $1.85
(tax included). BELL PHONE: Filbert 3395. Seats One Week in Advance.

Coming March 10th—VINCENT LOPEZ—and his Celebrated Orchestra

29. Another promotion of Breitbart in New York City

In February 1924 he set out on another tour - touring in twelve American cities. This time all his performances were advertised as the arrival of Superman of the Ages. At that time something very important, maybe even the most important to preserve the memory of Zishe had already happened. First in Cleveland and later in Toronto his performances were watched by two nine-year-old's.

Few years later, they would start their studies in the same school, and came up with the idea to create the figure who was an invincible hero. The inspiration might have been memories from childhood told among friends about a man who could break chains, and was called the Jewish Superman, Superman of the Ages and King of Iron. Any expert on the adventures of Clark Kent, Superman knows for sure about the two boys.

But let's go back to Zishe's stay in the USA. He chose New York as his American home and lived in Manhattan at 1819 Broadway (today Columbus Circle). By that time, New York was a large metropolis that was a city where politics, art, cinema, science and culture were connected. People full of inspiration and hope for a better future were flocking to it. For some it became a springboard for success, for others it is a place of failure. It was intimidating with his greatness and breadth, it never falls asleep, living forever with something new and something special and it has been from the moment in which it was created.

In America, Zishe's exploits aroused curiosity, but he also received criticism for his actions.

Dr. Morris Fishbein of the American Medical Association accused him of ... "anti-Americanism". Breitbart recommended to the future strongmen a dietary regime based on consuming raw vegetables while warning against eating too much milk and meat. Fishbein made an official protest to the citizenship and immigration office because this was against the current dietary thought.

By then, however, Zishe had already achieved star status. From his office in New York he managed a correspondence course for physical fitness. It is believed that the course he developed - a guide for athletes - was the first professional physical fitness program ever created. Orders for his regime were huge. The physical fitness correspondence course consisted of printed booklet on which featured a photo of Breitbart, above it was an inscription: "Superman of the Ages, the world's largest health builder, strength, muscle". When writing or phoning about getting the booklet, you had to ask for "SUPERMAN!"

DENTIST SAYS STRONG MAN WHO BITES IRON CHAINS IN TWO IS NOT SPOOFING THE PUBLIC

Breitbart, the strong man from Poland, is treating Brooklynites to an unusual demonstration of powerful feats. He bends heavy iron bands in fantastical designs and chews automobile links. All this is going on at the Orpheum Theatre where the "Iron Man" is being featured this week.

There having been some intimation that perhaps Breitbart was "spoofing" the public, a representative of the "Citizen" to-day sought out a well-known local dentist, who appeared on the stage at the Orpheum during the strong man's act as a witness to his almost unbelievable feats.

Breitbart's gums are in a perfect condition and his mouth is very healthy," said the dentist. "He is enabled to perform his extraordinary feats because he has developed his mastication muscles to a high state of perfection. The real strain lies not on the teeth, therefore but on the muscles of his jaw."

Exhibiting a link of an automobile chain which Breitbart bit in two in his presence, the dentist continued. "It took Breitbart between three and four minutes to bite this chain in two, and he accomplished it only by the tremendous power in his jaws and continual performance of his present act will undoubtedly tell on the peridental membrane

BALTIMORE NEWS

MARYLAND STRONG MAN ACCEPTS CRITIC'S CHALLENGE--AND WINS

By KENNETH W. BARR.

The laugh's on us. We're licked and we've got to admit it.

Here's the long and short of it. Monday afternoon we went to the Maryland. The headliner is Breitbart, billed as the world's strongest man. He treated wrought iron with the same ordinary people bend fence wire. And he purported to bite through iron chains.

We were only skeptical about the last feat, and said so in our review. It was simply a case of "being from Missouri." Many other folks in the audience felt the same way about it. Well, Herr Breitbart accepted our challenge yesterday--and won. Hence this story.

We presented the iron-jawed phenomenon with two different grades of steel chain of one-sixteenth-inch thickness. He wouldn't attempt the galvanized specimen. Nor did he attempt to bite through the other chain at any other place other than the joint. But he did tear two welded links apart, one in our presence.

Breitbart admitted he used iron chains of varying sizes on the stage. That being the case, his feat of separating a steel link is even more remarkable.

We were interested enough to take a chance on putting a finger inside of that massive jaw. There is a double set of bones making his jaw just twice as strong as that of any ordinary mortal. Furthermore, his front teeth are fully one-quarter-inch thick. Ours are just one-fourth as much.

Breitbart is returning for another Baltimore engagement in February.

Columbus Dispatch,
March 11, 1924.

From Providence Bulletin,
September 23, 1923.

Most Amazing Demonstration of Strength Ever Seen

The most amazing demonstration of physical strength ever seen on the stage is that of Breitbart, the European wonder, who appears at Keith's this week in one of the best headline acts of the season. He is touring the circuit after tremendous success at Keith's New York Hippodrome. Words fail, you must see him.

GREATEST STRONG MAN WORLD HAS EVER SEEN

A capacity audience at the E P J Albee Theatre yesterday afternoon thrilled to a series of astounding feats of strength and endurance by Breitbart, the Polish strong man. The demonstration is probably the most convincing of strength the var- city stage has seen.

30. Some of the articles discussing Zishe's abilities

So, he was just Superman! For the first time, a name was used to describe a man and became part of his legacy.

This excitement was also accompanied by unique press articles. It them Zishe begins to be called Superman by the general population. For example, one of them:

Breitbart, Modern Samson. The First American Appearance of Jewish Superman informs that he was born in a blacksmith's family in a small village in Poland. Zishe is called "Superman of Strength" and compared to Albert Einstein, and this is because only he among the Jews scattered around the world has a comparable large intellect similar to him!

Zishe was also sought after by other athletes. In Saratoga Springs, he met the extremely popular Jack Dempsey, one of the best-known athletes of the era. At the same time, he became a folk hero of sorts as poems and songs were written about him. In addition to Eastern Europe, these songs were also sung on streets of Manhattan's Lower East Side. The "Samson Potężny" (Powerful Samson) or "The Breitbart March" was sung by the people. Recognition, however, was not universal - he was not accepted everywhere, because of the common prejudices of that day many people would not believe that a Jew could not be the strongest man in the world.

In August 1924, he returned to Europe as an American citizen. This was most likely connected with problems that he had with American offices concerning advertising finances.

Telephone
Columbus 6506

Cable Address:
Superman-New York.

SIEGMUND BREITBART inc.

WORLD'S GREATEST BUILDER   **OF HEALTH, STRENGTH, MUSCLE**

1819 BROADWAY   NEW YORK CITY
GOTHAM BANK BLDG.—COLUMBUS CIRCLE

Mr; F. M. Cochran   Jan. 25, 1927.
High Point,
No. Car.

Dear Friend:

Let me congratulate you on sending in your measurement blank and enrollment for my course. This is the best decision you ever made and you will reap the benefits from it in a hundred ways.

I am herewith sending you your first lesson as well as the Introduction to my course. I am also sending you a loose leaf cover binder in which you should keep all the lessons, photographs, charts, etc. so that you may refer back to them from time to time. This binder will help to keep everything together, systematically and in order. In this way, when you have finished the course you will have a complete book on Physical Training, which, together with the special instructions that I will give you in my letters each week, will represent the greatest value you ever bought.

Now to begin with. I want you to read the Introduction very carefully. Then I want you to turn to Section A. of Lesson 1. and read this section through. Read what I have said about Moderation, Eating and Sleeping. It is very important for you to follow these instructions carefully, because the exercises will do you no good unless you do.

After you have read thru Section A, and fully absorbed the information given there, take the first exercise, which is BREATHING. Read the lesson all the way through and then perform the exercise as directed, following the numbers.

Don't think that just because these first exercises seem to be simple that I do not appreciate your present state of development. I have gone over your measurement blank very carefully, and I am giving you light work to start you off, but I don't want you to think for a minute that I won't give you the work just as fast as you can take it. I don't believe there has ever been any man that I could not help. I can help the man who has already acquired some degree of strength, as well as the man who is not so well developed. I want you to have full confidence

---

31. When writing or calling the Breitbart company you had to ask for "Superman"

58

32. An advertisement for the Breitbart Company

33. One of the most important Breitbart photographs in the USA.
It will be used as a drawing in the first Superman comic

AGAIN, ON THE NATIVE LAND, PREPARATIONS FOR FULFILLING THE GREAT MISSION

The year 1925 would be momentous for Zishe, who from the very beginning encountered a lot of extraordinary events. Unfortunately, however, he was the last in his life.

He appeared in Poland many times, where he was the biggest attraction and it was mainly for him that the audience came to the circus. To further emphasize the uniqueness of his performances, they were given special names. For example, performances in March were called the *"March Program"* and in April the *"April Program"*, although in principle their repertoire was unchanged.

On 14 March he received a lot of attention and was the most important guest at the ball in the "Palace" Hall at 9 Chmielna Street in Warsaw. The event was announced as extraordinary because "Every lady can dance with Breitbart! Take advantage of the opportunity! "On the same day he also took part in another ball combined with a concert, advertised, for the same as the one in which he announced his performance in it.

This popularity also did not sit well with some people who set out to malign him. On April 18, some of the newspapers informed readers that a day before in Warsaw, a leaflet was distributed there that reported a catastrophe in which he died that evening. In connection with this, crowds gathered in front of the Bristol Building where they wanted to check the above-mentioned rumor. Of course, they were left in the cold.

Upon returning to Europe he often visited Jewish sports clubs. Some of them could also have been said to have somewhat biblical roots. Since the destruction

61

34. Zishe performing his signature act in Krakow

of the Temple, it was the family that was the basic link ensuring the survival of Jewish identity. Creating groups - heroes' bands was an extension of this philosophy.

He also organized "The Breitbart Games". One of them took place in Lviv on the field of Ż.K.S. Hasmonei (The most popular Jewish soccer team), where Zishe gave evidence of his phenomenal strength to an audience of over 8,000, he donated his income to the House of Health for Jewish students.

Following this up, his visit to Vilnius was also a sensation. In front of the Łazar restaurant at Mickiewicza Street, a horse-drawn carriage stopped, from which Zishe got out in his original circus outfit. It was a preview of the performance of the newly opened Circus by Czesław Mroczkowski. The Jewish community prepared an ovation and waited in front of the restaurant until he finished eating dinner. Then the fans followed the horse-drawn carriage which took the strong man to the circus. The problem was that a growing number of crooks began selling counterfeit tickets to the circus and speculators began selling them at inflated prices.

35. Hasmanei Sports Club – Lwow

He developed a huge promotion and advertisement campaign, which to a large extent would make him such an extremely popular man.

Another great event was the performance of Zishe in Będzin, his mother's family's home town, which was one of his last performances. The stadium in Będzin was the pride of the Jewish community of Zagłębie, where the seat of the Jewish Gymnastic and Sports Society "Hakoach" was located. Tickets for the show sold like fresh rolls, and the lucky ones who managed to buy them impatiently began to ask, "What will our king show this time?" He dressed in his usual Roman costume when appearing in public, in a way that all Jews waited for and enjoyed most. He had a helmet on his head, a cloak with an embroidered Star of David on his body, and he looked like a Roman gladiator. Dressed in this manner, of course, he drove a chariot harnessed with steeds full of energy. Then he easily held the cart, where those stallions could not break free from his iron grip.

Later he performed in the circus of the Staniewski Brothers. One occasion in Bialystok in 1925 went down in history because that's where the most faithful fans of the strongman from the whole Central and Eastern European Jewish diasporas came. When the news spread through Bialystok that Zishe was arriving at the local station from Warsaw, crowds of people gathered there. As the athlete left the train he was welcomed by an orchestra in full gala, along with an appearance by the local rabbis. The enthusiastic crowd took Breitbart in their arms and pulled his carriage directly from the station. A specially decorated carriage took him to the hotel. From then on, the circus grounds were under siege. Everyone wanted to see a special number with their own eyes, which would only be performed in the Staniewski Circus (there are still photos from this unusual number). A special motorcycle track was built, which was placed on the strongman's chest and two people rode around on him. On the last day of the performances (and they lasted a week), the program was topped with chains brought by local skeptics who doubted the real strength of the athlete to tear them off. This number, not previously planned, often appeared in the repertoire of his other European or world performances.

36. The Maccabi Games that Zishe Breitbart supported

Everyone who tried to get involved in the Staniewski Circus needed to follow a certain level of presented skills, which they needed to match Breitbart's. "You had to have the strength of Zishe Breitbart and how he could bend horseshoes in his hands, to break chains to get into the circus of the Staniewski brothers at Ordynacka in Warsaw" - repeated by many known strongmen even winning a wrestling tournament. He was the star and the biggest attraction of this circus.

The year 1925 was the one in which he would officially get involved in politics. He wanted to be a symbol of the Zionist movement in Eastern Europe. He planned a trip to Palestine where he intended to act as a champion of the independent state of Israel. This was at a time when there was a growing Zionist movement in Europe and Poland for immigration to Israel. He even obtained the blessing of the Chief Rabbi of Poland for all activities in this direction. The Rabbi also called him the "New Samson". Breitbart wrote a congratulatory letter on the occasion of the opening in of the first university in the Land of Israel, in 1925, which was the Hebrew University located on the hill Mount Scopus in Jerusalem. He received an invitation to honor its opening. The trip was to take place after his performances in Poland, after the last one which was supposed to be that unlucky performance in Radom.

He believed that his performances would be remembered especially by young Jews, from whom the next generation of Maccabees will grow up. Maccabeus, a Hebrew hammer, in other words Juda Maccabeus, who led the Maccabi - the humble army of the Maccabees, which in 156 BC. defeated the Greek army. From then on, Maccabi became a symbol of the Jewish people's struggle. At the beginning of the 20th century, the "Maccabi" sports clubs were established within the Polish lands, with a strong Zionist color. All Zionist youths were associated in them. In addition to the organization of numerous sports events, training exhibitions also raised funds for future settlement in Palestine. It was for these new settlers who, in Zishe Breitbart's plans, were to teach the strength and reason of future creators of the independent state of Israel. His dream was to create a kind of international sport league for Jews, an organization that would have greater political consequences: he imagined that it would include military training, which would ultimately facilitate the creation of a Jewish army that would be able to protect themselves in Palestine. He admired Włodzimierz Żabotyński's representative of the radical trend in the Zionist movement, which initiated the creation of the Jewish Legion.

37. Zishe bending iron. Note the "centurion" costume he is wearing.

Zishe, as we would say today, was socially involved. In Lviv, Breitbart's Evening was arranged in the halls of the "National House". The hero himself gave away various souvenirs to the ladies during the meeting. Income from the event, which was limited to a small number of people, was intended to be used to support the sick and poor Jews in Lviv.

More and more he was seen as a hero, the embodiment of the strength of the Jewish nation. On more than one occasion he was heard to say, "If I see an anti-Semite, I give him a sincere warning. If he does not give in, I will break him in half like a match. "

In this way he reacted to anti-Semitic provocations. He was a wonderful child of the Jewish community, who identified with the "street" and lower classes.

It was said that Jewish families hung his portrait in their houses and prayed for his successes. He continued to perform in costumes that made him look like a legendary or mythological strongman. In one performance in Krakow, for example he paraded in the venue escorted by men in stylized ancient Roman costumes

Still people did not believe his strength was real and tried by any means to undermine his extraordinary abilities. It also happened that while reporting on his performances, lies were written, and during their lifetime attempts were made to disrupt his performances by trying to provoke him. On July 21, 1925, one week before the tragic events with Zishe in Radom, he appeared in Bielsko in the sports stadium "Hakoah". It was recorded that a large Jewish crowd filled this square to admire how the "second Samson". The strongman had to perform all the shows on his own specially prepared devices. This created unrest among some of the audience, because of the various tricks and machinations. Breitbart offered $1,000 to a willing daredevil who would repeat even one of his numbers. Two well-known amateur gymnasts, Bomschn and Rozkwas, took up the challenge, declaring that they would duplicate all his routines. According to the press, Breitbart and the Jewish committee prevented the daredevils from the stage. The part of the audience consisting of Germans and Poles began to whistle. There was confusion, the police had to intervene, which saved the whole situation. Zishe retreated to the locker room, and the audience carried the two brave daredevils on their hands. However, it is not known to the end whether this incident was a kind of provocation aimed at discrediting the skills of a strongman. Even if the audience gave an ovation to the two men who took up the challenge and did not do anything at all. Whether or not Zishe's strength is natural and true was asked of the famous martial arts champion, Władysław Pytlasiński, extremely popular in Europe and America.

"Is Mr. Breitbart really a phenomenal strongman?" This is the question asked by one of the newspapers to Pytlasinski, at the same time handing him iron bars and figures bent out of them. The athletics expert, as he was then called, replied that:

"Breitbart is undoubtedly stronger than ordinary mortals, but iron in his hands has been bent by many people."

He quoted the name of Sandow from England, who with one hand raised pianos and horses, the athletes of Lutów and Garkowienka, who were bending ten-inch pipes at the back of their necks. He divided athletes into various categories: those who are wrestlers or weightlifting specialists or those who, with their natural strength, can stand out in each of these categories. He stressed that much can be achieved by using special art. He developed a way of performing these unlikely demonstrations while intelligently using his strength. In the case of Breitbart, he explained this with an extraordinary force expressed in lifting heavy weights on his chest by skillfully shifting the center of gravity to his knees. Bones of the human leg in the vertical direction withstand a great load. At the same time, he suggested that:

"Mr Breitbart's walk indicates that he is abusing his legs. It's bad and it certainly would not have gone one kilometer. "

He also believed that these performances do not belong to athletics at all. They are simply "tour de forces" - circus shows. He also suggests that in the wrestling or boxing match the average athlete would easily defeat Breitbart. After picking up by the nickname in the newspaper, he did not call him "Samson II" a great physical example of the Jews. It cannot be concealed, however, that in this press interview you can feel jealousy towards Zishe. Jealousy for his incredible achievements. Pytlashinski added that he once bent iron on the back of his neck in Odessa, the thickness of the rim from the wheels.

Besides, the press, was not helpful to the strongman, sometimes gave very poor coverage of his performances. For example, during one of the exhibitions in Łódź, the strongman was unpleasantly surprised. Before beginning of the routine for bending a number of the long iron bars, an inconspicuous young man entered the arena copied the same routine, including bending the iron bar in his mouth and bent the iron hoops rom inferior material. Upset, Zishe almost beat a serious competitor and the police put an end to the whole event.

DEATH OF "NEW SAMSON"

During the performances in Radom at the end of July 1925, there was an unfortunate accident when he performed one of the standard numbers: during the performance he pounded a spike through five-inch-thick oak boards using only his bare hands leaning against one of his knees. During this performance he accidently pierced his knee. Zishe most likely used too much force to hit the spike. The spike was rusty and caused a blood infection that caused gangrene. An infection set in on the untreated wound, the leg was soon amputated, but the disease progressed. The other leg was amputated to protect against the rest of the body. Later, the sepsis became more involved. The procedure and the treatment process according to the *Leipziger Judische Zeitung* were taken care of by Rabbi Dr. Meier Hildesheimer. In total, he underwent ten operations, but it did not help. He died in Berlin two months after the accident on October 12, when he was only 32 years old.

38. Radom, where Breitbart had his last performance

Death occurred as a result of an injury suffered during one of the simplest circus tricks. To pierce the board with a nail it is not necessary to have Herculean strength. Hitting a nail through the board is first of all about mastering the impact technique, which is not so difficult. Smacking the head of the nail so as not to damage the hand should be put between the second and third finger. The impact should come straight from above. If you use all the energy to break the board, the trick will surely work. This however, emphasizes the need to carefully wrap the nail head so that you do not get injured. Zishe did not foresee the fact that by performing this standard number for himself the nail would pierce his knee. The strongman who dragged the wagons full of people with chains or raised a small elephant, he used to treat this number with sticking the nail probably as a daily bread and did not concentrate too much during its implementation.

The newspaper *Słowo*, published in Poland in Vilnius, posted a short article about the accident. The information in it is extremely interesting. Before the next proposed eleventh operation, the victim had to call the family, but also to "a number of his supporters and friends in Warsaw so that they would send a delegation to the aforementioned tzadik from Radzymin who lived in Falenica near Warsaw". What was the matter in this case? Zishe wanted to receive a blessing from him, he had previously commit and promised to provide eleven sacks of flour for the poor from whom the matzah would be baked. Despite several reminders from the tsaddik, he never did follow through on this. He believed that this was associated with the painful accident and he believed that in this way the finger of God reached him by not keeping the word. He wanted the delegation to soften the heart of the tsaddik and obtain his forgiveness, so that after he regained his health, would immediately perform the promise he had made. The delegation headed by Ikon Isakson was received by the tsaddik, where he received forgiveness and the assurance of prayers for Zishe. Before the next operation the strongman lived in the conviction that he would finally regain his health, and this opinion was shared by most of his fellow believers. One may wonder why a strong man who helped the poor did not follow through on this simple task. Had he simply forgotten about it with everything else going on in his world? Were there any other reasons unknown to us? A month after his death, Breitbart's biography was published, which he co-authored as: *Mayn Lebens Geshikhte* (*History of My Life*). However, it was an unfinished work, which was emphasized by his co-author, Ben Kuscher and therefore it is not a completely faithful reflection of his life. This item cannot be treated as a complete or credible source about Zishe. There is a lot of unverified information in it, some information written with the fans in mind.

39. Postcard depicting the death of Zishe Breitbart

Postcards depicting the last moments of Breitbart's life and those documenting his funeral ceremonies were very popular. For many people, Breitbart's sudden and unexpected death was considered a publicity stunt to be expected by the showmanship of the New Samson. Many saw his death as part of Breitbart's authentic links to the biblical Samson and proof that he was him! Why? The story of Samson has a deep moral and religious sense. Samson does not rise to the task God has entrusted to him as a result of his own recklessness. For some, the history of his life shows how the great gifts of God can be wasted, because he wasted his gifts. Death took place as a result of: bad luck, bad luck, unhappiness, conspiracy of all bad circumstances. However, it was possible to avoid this tragedy. Zishe's recklessness was to disregard the threat posed by the performance of this simple circus number.

Soon other voices were heard, which raised the question whether he was really the "King of Iron" or as it as some had said "The King of Bluff". The Vienna press made a great deal about it, as it was there that he began his global career. One man, an editor named Reich, in the Austrian magazine *Die Stunde*, who repeatedly took part, as an expert of a special commission examining the strengths of the strongman, wrote that what he did was indeed opposed to physical laws. The Commission, in which he worked with the utmost care and severity, tested these

71

extraordinary skills beyond the scope of human capabilities. For example, it was not possible to explain how the strongman could pound nails with his teeth. The editor wrote that they gathered experts in various fields, dentists who checked whether Breitbart's teeth contained any iron cutting material. Metal experts even took them to the laboratories to study their properties. In conclusion, the editor informed that absolutely nothing was found that could indicate that there was any fraud in it. Zishe never revealed where his power came from. It seemed strange to him that such an unusual person could die as a result of infection from a nail driven into the body. However, Zishe's skills and the whole phenomenon remained unintelligible to this journalist. It seemed unlikely that man would have such abilities. Then the name "Steal King" began to appear.

He was buried in Berlin at Adass Jisroel Cementery, in the presence of a huge crowd of people. The following text was read over his grave:

> *"On the body Your great - black clods of earth*
> *Graved gravediggers scattered.*
> *They were bent over you, terrified, mute.*
> *The spades fell out of their hands - they turned their faces away.*
> *Because they knew that the thunderbolt had died out today*
> *A marble column that fate crushed !!! "*

After his death, his estate continued to prosper for many years through business ventures he had set up in his lifetime. His name continued to be used on mail and correspondence courses on physical culture to look as if Breitbart was still alive. In 1931, the US Federal Trade Commission detected this fraud and banned this activity.

In 1928, the writer Jecheskiel Mosze Neumann (Najman) proposed a fantasy film scenario entitled "Life of Zishe Breitbart" in the *Film Velt Daily*. The script was written in Warsaw three years after the death of the strongman. In this story Zishe meets Samson, who considers him with his twenty-century incarnation.

"Hello, my friend in the twentieth century" - that's how Samson turns into Zishe. The strongman is confused, and he asks Samson where he is now. He gets the answer that "in your strength and heart, my friend." Further, Breitbart learns that he is now to defend the Jews against persecution. Some of these scenarios were later used by Werner Herzog in the film production, *The Invincible*.

Even as late as the 1930's, songs were sung about him in Manhattan. George Eisen, the author of, among other books: *Jewish history and the ideology of*

40. Zishe preforming on a raised platform before a large crowd in Krakow. He is wearing his Centurion uniform

modern sport: Approaches and Interpretations, writes that from his childhood in Hungary, he remembers stories of the strongman's exploits, who broke chains with his bare hands and is known to him from the expression, "Do not pretend to be Breitbart." Interestingly, he claims that this saying is even known there today!

FACTS, MYTHS AND LEGENDS ABOUT ZISHE'S LIFE

Breitbart's biographies became the source of the folk legend. Unfortunately, none of them containing real information about him about him. They contain a lot of information that is contradictory and false. They are important, however, in that their message was objective, when they described his extraordinary physical strength, his involvement in the affairs of the Jewish people or the help he provided to people in need of help.

He certainly never denied his Jewish origin and always performed with the national white and blue banner, not paying attention to the fact that the majority of people who saw his shows did not profess his religion. Photographs primarily depict his pensive expression and a spiritual look. The folk legend itself creates a generous, disinterested, socially vulnerable character who used his strength for good purposes from childhood. However, in all these stories about Zishe's life, common features inevitably appear. He is always portrayed as a person who helps poor and oppressed people and is called "Iron Kings", "Modern Samson".

As far as we know he was faithful to his wife in his lifetime, who he loved very much (it is also very interesting when we remember the comic Superman and his great love Lois Lane).

From his childhood Zisha dreamed about becoming the Strongman Samson and Bar-Kochba. It emphasizes the strongman's obsession with the creation of a Jewish army that will build independent Israel. Though many considered them naive dreams, this idea was taken by a group of politicians fascinated by his personality. Among them, it has been said were Włodzimierz Żabotyński and Chaim Weizman. Irgun also inspired these ideas - this is how the clandestine army fighting for independence of Israel was defined.

This is extremely important if we are looking for features in common with the comic Superman.

Various stories about the life of Breitbart often consist of situations that are probably somewhat stretched, twisted, or even those that did not take place. If they are carefully examined, there are often many inaccuracies in them that exclude well-known facts. It was probably taken from authentic events that were passed from word of mouth, and unwritten on an ongoing basis are always misrepresented and changed slightly from person to person. All of them were basically created shortly before or after the tragic death of Zishe. He did not have to comment on them or even explain since he did not know about them. Perhaps these errors and inaccuracies also arose from inaccurate translations and understanding of proper names, i.e. idioms most often translated from Polish into English. Therefore, very often his life is slightly mythological, but maybe even more so thanks to the linkage to the biblical Samson.

According to Gisela and Ditmar Winklers, in the book, *Allez Hop*[15], his mother would tell him that in the first year of his life she had noticed the extraordinary strength he had. In turn, his father was said that everyone in the family always had great strength.

When he was three years old, his mother would send him with food to his father's forge. It was then that a metal grille was about to crush him and he freed himself from its weight. A year later he systematically helped his father at work where he would spend a few hours working in the forge. Their publication also states that at the age of five, the family moved to a new home on Jerusalem Street. It was already more magnificent and more convenient than the previous one at Berezin Street. The Winklers say that the future strongman was born in Łódź - Strikow, so once again Stryków is treated as a district of Lodz. Indeed, in Zishe's youth, there was a street in Łódź, Jerozolimska, but there was no Berezin street, maybe it was a distorted name of Brzezińska Street, because it was a similar name.

There is also the often referenced first school to which he attended, which was a "cheder". Such a school also existed in Stryków. It was in this school that Zishe first demonstrated his strength in defense of the weak. In the schools he attended, he would take breakfast from wealthier colleagues and share them among the poorer.

One of the stories about the early years of the life of the strongman mentions a Rabbi Meisel Eliyahu Hayim. Indeed, in the years 1873 - 1912 he was a rabbi in Łódź, who enjoyed great recognition there, especially among the Hasid's. It was in those years that the Jewish community grew from ten thousand to one hundred

15. Gisela and Ditmar Winklers. *Allez hopp durch die Welt. Aus dem Leben berühmter Akrobaten*. Henschelverlag (1977)

41. Zishe, early in his career

and sixty thousand, being more than one-third of the entire city community. He is credited with the establishment of a Talmud Torah professional school for young men. Zishe first began his education there and became fascinated with this rabbi.

According to the Winklers, one day as a youth of about twelve he supposedly went to Łódź with *Zielona Solomansky`s Circus* or *Circus Underwater[16]*. At that time there was a strong man who raised twenty people and broke iron hoops. The twelve-year old was delighted with the strength of this strongman. Soon, another small circus was coming to town, this time to Grzybowska Street (no street like this was ever in Łódź). It was with this circus that he was supposed to started performing, not as a strongman, but as ... a clown! This job was offered to him without understanding his extraordinary skills. Before the performance he had to train with horses and where his great strength gained attention. He was then promoted to Yiddish actor. Almost at once in this position, he was entrusted with a role in the play *Bar Kochba* where he played the character of Yehuda. In addition to acting skills, he was able to show off his extraordinary strength. He was then offered a permanent job in this circus. This story probably influenced Zishe's false birth date.

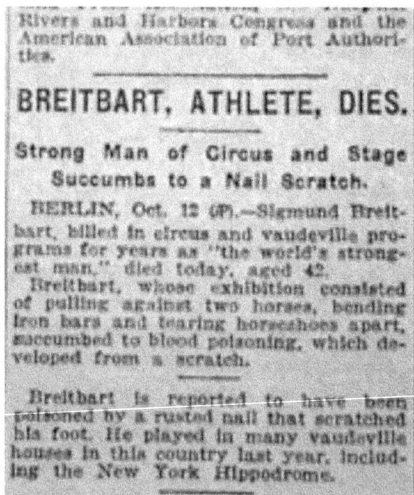

Rivers and Harbors Congress and the American Association of Port Authorities.

BREITBART, ATHLETE, DIES.

Strong Man of Circus and Stage Succumbs to a Nail Scratch.

BERLIN, Oct. 12 (P).—Sigmund Breitbart, billed in circus and vaudeville programs for years as "the world's strongest man," died today, aged 42.

Breitbart, whose exhibition consisted of pulling against two horses, bending iron bars and tearing horseshoes apart, succumbed to blood poisoning, which developed from a scratch.

Breitbart is reported to have been poisoned by a rusted nail that scratched his foot. He played in many vaudeville houses in this country last year, including the New York Hippodrome.

42. Notice of Zishe's death in the New York Herald

Yet in another version of the story about the circus, which supposed was to appear in Bałuty, which was the mostly Jewish district of Lodz. This is where the strongman came to get his first job. He was supposed said that he was fourteen. Zishe supposedly impress the audience because most of them were already bored of the wrestling show in the repertoire called "French".

There is also another address given for the family's residence in Łódź at 8 Smoliar Street (there was never such a street or a similarly sounding name in this city). In the same story there appears a completely

16. Gisela Winkler, *Tye*, Berlin, 1998, p.41

fictional and never occurring event about the pogrom of Jews in Łódź in 1888. Zishe was supposed to be five years old then, which is also untrue because he was not in the world yet. However, the pogroms supposedly reached a place near Łódź called Starowieshtch, which again, seems like a distorted name for Stryków which is referred to as a district of Łódź. The author derives this from the alleged former using the name Starowieshtch as Starye Veshtchi. According to this story, the family's lives were threatened during the pogrom. Meanwhile, history says something completely different. It was at this time that the Jews fleeing from the Muscovy district were massively resettled to Łódź, because the pogroms took place in that Russian city. Łódź was a city considered a safe city for Jews the Russian Empire.

Still another source gives the family's street address as the whole Zgerz Ghetto in Łódź. Perhaps he meant the town of Zgierz bordering Łódź or it is a shortened and incorrect name of Zgierska Street in Łódź. The author was the Paris correspondent for the *Buenos Aires Yiddish Daily Di Presse* newspaper, Abraham Shulman. In this issue of this newspaper from 18 January 1957, he published an interesting portrait of Zishe - *King Iron*, a Jewish strongman in the Parisian Museum Honors hanging in the Palais Chaillot. The author wrote this article more than thirty years after Zishe's death by collecting various information that is often untested.

There was also a story written about him by Dr. A. H. Kober in 1927. According to him, he was called the "Iron King" as early as 1917, because this was the point when he started to be well known. He also describes the meeting that took place in Cologne between Breitbart and the phenomenal strong woman Katia Sandwiną. He was supposed to be the greatest strongman then, and she was the biggest strongwoman. They performed together in Cologne in 1919.

He also mentioned where the strong man lived. The house was called Villa Breitbart, which was purchased in 1922. The estate left by a strongman was estimated at 80,000 Goldmark. The author puts a rhetorical question: "Will anyone someday and wherever come with similar skills to Breitbart, or will he always remain the only and unique King of Iron".

Rafael Schermann was able to see him in the USA. In the memorial about the strongman posted in *Prager Tagblatt* on 13 October 1925, however, the incorrect information was given about the accident which turned out to be fatal occurred while performing at the *Berlin Variete* at forty-two years of age.

The author also draws attention to his extraordinary role in the art of Goldfaden Bar-Kochba. He also talks about the regiment of soldiers who would be like Zishe Breitbart in the future.

43. In Washington, pulling a wagon of fifty people with a chain between his teeth

During his stay in America at the turn of 1923/24 information in the press appeared to say that he was born in 1887.

It was also then that the next confrontation between Breitbart and Hanussen occurred, just as unexpectedly as it had been in Vienna in less than a year. The confrontation between them took place at Gartner's Restaurant on Broadway. They were both going to perform there. The dispute between them ended quickly - it was largely suspended thanks to the director of the center where they met, who did not want any scandals, such as took place in Vienna. Both men came to mutual agreement and the animosity disappeared. The strong man agreed to the suggestions of his antagonist, concerning the performance of certain circus numbers. Thus, Zishe proved that his strength is not imagined or pretended.

In Washington, he performed a number by pulling the platform with a chain held in his mouth, with 75 people on it.

In one of the American newspapers in 1924, it was written that his father was still working as a blacksmith when he was 65, while his grandmother lived 113 and his grandfather 119. The information about the length of grandparents' life is certainly untrue.

Erroneous information on the date and place of birth is also provided by most encyclopedias. For example, *Lexikon Judisches: Łódź 1883, Encyclopedia - The Universal Jewish: Łódź 1883 or American Hebrew*.

An article was dedicated to him in the Warsaw press by Menachem Kipnis, where he described the "death of a Jewish hero". According to him, every Jewish citizen wanted to come to Breitbart, who defended a group of Jews from hooligans when he was nine. He also quotes the opinion that in one of the plays of a Jewish writer from Poland, Sholema (Szoloma) Ascha Montke Ganev, the heroes are people from Breitbart's surroundings.

"Everyone wanted to see a Jewish hero" - he concludes his article. He also writes that all songs, or stories about the strong man helped create his legend, which everyone in the world would be telling for many years.

Is not this an extraordinary statement? Is this not a preview of birth in the near future in the form of the Superman comic book?

FOLLOWERS AND CHARLATANS

Zishe grew to become a great hope for Jews scattered around the world. It was believed that his time was really coming. When he died so suddenly, they knew that dreams connected with him would never be fulfilled. No songs, stories have replaced the longing for "New Samson," which no longer exists. The popular legend needed a successor.

Several days after Breitbart's death, in Berlin there were several popular exhibitions of strength in the local streets. They consisted of a man resembling Breitbart who tried to imitate his unusual numbers.

"Zishe Breitbart's rival: cabman Mojsze Hoc from Ciechanów was the healthiest Jew in Poland. When he took an ox under his arm, it could not break free. He chose to compact iron from Warsaw and tear the chains, in repetition of the same routines as Zishe Breitbart. April 25, 1926."

A photograph with this annotation was recently presented in Poland at the Jewish Historical Institute, and its author is the pre-war Polish currency exchanger and journalist Menachem Kipnis. He researched and performed folk songs of Polish Jews, so those songs about Breitbart were not alien to him. The photograph depicted a man standing in the middle of a paved yard with long boots and a cap with a visor. Behind him, with a low build, the cabman is visible. The man is wearing a tight jacket and gives the impression of being tired. The main character of the photo is Mojsze Hoc, cabman from Ciechanów. He was to be the second Breitbart. Was he really that strong? This comparison came from Kipnis's pen, for which Zishe was also great. It is more ironic than a real fact. Perhaps Hoc was actually a physically strong man, but Breitbart was only one. And never again will anyone match his exploits. Hoc seems to be a simple man who lacks even the grace and delicacy that characterized Zishe's character.

In the same year another copycat appeared. The show was brought to Białystok by an American of Polish descent, the strongman Stefan "Ursus" Piatkowski. Without believing in his skills, he was timidly styled as the "King of Iron" like

44. After Zishe's death there were many imitators

Zishe before. His beat-up number was a fight with an enraged bull and then being buried underground for three hours - as it was announced without the flow of air! During the next act he had a car driven over him. To the misfortune of the man, the car stopped unexpectedly on him - this was a tragedy. Piątkowski with a crushed left side of his body was transported to the hospital. He eventually returned to his performances, but he avoided the most difficult ones. In 1937 he was defeated by Stanisław Radwan, a sailor from Krakow. In the Maritime Station Hall in Gdynia, they competed with each other: a young sailor of the navy and, as it was announced, "King of Iron". They alternately cut thicker chains, twisted and straightened nails or hammers, breaking boulders lying on their breasts. Everything to the point where Radwan, holding the bit in his teeth, would not allow the horses to move. Piatkowski was dumbstruck, he took off his master belt and put on the hip of a 30-year-old sailor. This is how this strongman was born, who was given the nickname "Iron Jaws". On the decks of ships, on which he served in the ranks, he participated in strength duels on a mat. He defeated strongmen from Europe, Africa and Asia. He successfully fought on German and Soviet cruisers hosting a courtesy visit in Gdynia. It had an amazing propaganda effect - Poles loved him. Apparently, during World War II, when he

84

was in the camp as a prisoner, when one of the Nazis stuck a gun in his mouth, he gritted his teeth and bit off the barrel. In the case of Radwan, however, the origin of his unbelievable strength can be explained: he had a double number of teeth or a hyper-donation. After the war, luck smiled and he came to the USA. He was looked after by none other than the famous Polish strongman, among others the 1925 heavy-weight wrestling world champion from Philadelphia - Zbyszko Cyganiewicz[17]. Zishe Breitbart also helped this American legend. He found work for him in a circus with which he performed for five years. He was called the "King of Iron and Steel", and even went to Hollywood.

There were also those who tried to gain something for themselves, preying on the popularity of the strongman of Strykow. A year after Breitbart's death, *Ilustrowany Kuryer Codzienny* in Poland, reported that a scandal erupted in Lodz. Thanks to a man named Jack Bronx, a strongman who has come to be known as the "King of Iron" said he was stronger than Zishe and, like him, was able to break horseshoes, bend iron or hammer nails into powerful logs of a tree. He tried to take the place of the then legendary Zishe. His performances gathered large crowds of people especially during one of the performances in Łodz. While the strongman demonstrated his extraordinary skills, he was unexpectedly joined by the infamous young man, seventeen-year-old Max Helrich, who was learning the profession of a shoemaker. To everyone's amazement, he grabbed one of the horseshoes and bent it without a problem. There was silence. A moment later, he grabbed the big nail and drove it into the board with ease. He explained to the astonished audience that the horseshoes were made of tin, which bent like plasticine. It also turned out that the plate, in which the strongman was fixing the nails, was actually cardboard. It is not known why Helrich decided to perform such a farcical act. Maybe he knew the cheater before or noticed that the items are counterfeits. In any case, a big scandal broke out, the audience demanded a refund for tickets, and the "strongman" wanted to escape before he was lynched. The police finally saved him, but he was accused of "cheeky cheating." It turned out that he was actually Jakub Buk - a Jewish porter from Warsaw.

In 1927, the press reported that the police in Krakow arrested a group of con men who copied Brietbart's original act. The scammers were visited many cities in Poland where they performed as Breitbart. Staying in hotels and restaurants they did not pay bills, and when it was discovered that they were ordinary frauds they would immediately leave for another city. They found easy pickings especially in the Eastern Borderlands of Poland, squares, squares, and backyards which were full of young boys imitating Breitbart and trying to match his strength.

---

17. Real name was Władysław Cyganiewicz

The spirit and memory of Zishe remained alive for some time. In 1927, a Jewish athlete named Possof, who was a "Maccabi" instructor in Frankfurt am Main was famous in Poland. He became famous for stopping two cars with a strength of "64 horsepower". "The performances of the phenomenal athlete – who was Jewish, incited great interest among Jewish circles. The Jewish masses in Warsaw, who still had a deep respect for the tragically deceased strongman Breitbart, enthusiastically greet every performance of the athlete - an intellectual with a sympathetic Semitic face full of enthusiasm, seeing in him the symbol of their lost pride - Breitbart."

During the same year in Lviv, the performances of eleven-year-old Mishko Geller called "Youth Breitbart" were advertised and surprised many with is demonstrations of physical strength and telepathic experiments. At this point, it may be time for a small digression. Less than twenty years later, a man of above-average telepathic abilities will be born in Tel Aviv. I wonder if this is some relative of Geller who was compared to Breitbart or just a coincidence.

There were other phenoms like a fourteen-year-old boy who called himself, Samson, because he was lifting extremely heavy objects, as well as another named Samson Brown. In turn he often performed and dressed as Breitbart and tried to copy his routines.

In June 1929, in Lublin, the Zishe brothers Gerson and Josef had been anticipated to arrive in Poland for months. But, it turned out that imposters were impersonating them. Gerson came to Lublin to explain the situation and as a result ... he was persuaded for a joint performance with the impostors.

In the 1960's in England, the street artist – Polish strongman Stefan Siatowski was extremely popular. He tried to be the perfect copy of Zishe. He was declared a "Samson" and "The Strongest Man of the World". His outfit also referred to the Roman gladiator. Anyone who managed to repeat one of his feats was promised a certain amount of money. His most important number was lifting weights. They were not, however, huge barbells or other heavy items, and the bent kitchen wooden chair. The task was to raise the chair sideways with the seat held horizontally in a mechanically unfavorable position. No one has ever been able to repeat this act. A Volleyball team was accompanied by a presenter with the stage name Delilah (in the Bible a woman with that name was Samson's partner). He could also bend rods and nails, which he also pounded with his bare hand in a hard board. His work was described by David Webster in the book Sons Of Samson vol 2. However, not only did he imitate Breitbart - almost every extraordinary strongman gave himself the nickname the King of Steel. Since

45. Gus Waldorf battles a bear

Zishe was given his famous nickname as the "King of Iron" or "King of Steel" or "Man of Steel" this was now applied to almost every player who sports strength! Similarly, with the term "Samson", many add this title to your name or surname!

In 1949, an official boxing match between the man and ... a brown bear took place in the USA. The rival of the animal was Gus Waldorf. Despite the fact that the bear was fighting in a muzzle and had limited freedom of movement, he won the duel.

Was it a reference to a similar duel that Zishe had once fought?

THE FATE OF THE
BREITBARTS - BRAJTBARTS

As a famous man did Zishe, return to visit his hometown? What happened to his family? Was anyone in Stryków aware of who he was?

A coverage of performances at the Łódź Odeon in Poland has been preserved. "Breitbart lies on nails, lifts the road with horses, people, vehicles." As the strongman's performance was advertised in the *Republika* newspaper.

There is no information on whether he returned to visit Stryków.

Everything seems to indicate that the family later moved to Łódź, which seems reasonable given their improved financial status. However, it is difficult to determine the exact date of this event. The reason for moving out of Stryków could have also been for another reason.

In 1914, the tsarist authorities forbade the use of Yiddish. The tsarist administration, fearing that the Jews could cooperate with the German occupation authorities, began their forced deportations to those places belonging to Russia that were not involved in the war which resulted in about 500,000 Jews being displaced. In turn, when German troops entered Kingdom of Poland in 1916, living conditions in the zones of Jewish settlement became unbearable. The tsarist authorities, once again fearing that the desperate Jewish citizens would cooperate with the Germans and Austrians, so they abolished restrictions on Jewish settlement, allowing Jews to settle in the territory of the entire Russian Empire. At the same time, publishing in Hebrew or Yiddish was forbidden in public.

From the old registration books of Stryków we have learned that Zishe's father lived in Łódź in 1918, but his son Aron Szlama (the oldest, Zishe's brother) was a resident of Stryków, so only part of the family moved to Lodz.

After the death of the strongman, the Polish press appeared in Łódź and reported that "the son of Łódź passed away" - this is of course not true. "He was 42 years old and supposedly he was born somewhere on Drewnowska street." It was there that he began his great adventure as a member of a traveling circus troupe. This is also incorrect information as was that "war with Germany surprised him". Why did the contemporary Polish press still repeat the wrong information? Most likely it was due to inadequate information and reproduction of unverified sources. Zishe died in a time when his popularity was at its peak and he simply did not have time to read everything written about him which included verifying false information.

Why was the name Stryków also distorted, describing it as one of the districts of Łódź?

In Breitbart's childhood, Łódź was a Polish city under Russian rule and it was still developing rapidly as an industrial center which was known and recognized in Europe. The city was known mainly for the production of cotton. It was inhabited by Poles, rich Jewish and Germans merchants, a garrison of Russian soldiers and their families. That is why it was made of Łódź citizens of Antoni Cierplikowski called - the king of hairdressers and Max Factor (Max Factor) creator of the cosmetics network. They came from Stryków, Sieradz and Zduńska Wola – all small towns belonging to Russia at that time, and about whom people in Western Europe, and certainly no one in the United States had heard of. Abroad, they were most often regarded as people from Łódź.

This is how it is to this day and maybe there is no wonder, because it is Lodz that has people who have a huge impact on ... the contemporary image of the majority of people! Some of the best-known inhabitants were: Rodeo Ben (Bernard Lichtenstein) creator of the Wrangler brand, Jacek Trzmiel founder of Commodore, Zdzisław Starostecki co-founder of the Patriot missile system, Jan Karski, the first courier to inform US President Franklin Delano Roosevelt about the persecution of Jews, Dżigan and Schumacher a pair of Jewish comedians. We should also mention Colonel Janie Kowalewski, whose all-cipher system was interested from all of countries participating in World War II. The ancestors of two architects Frank Gehry and Daniel Libeskind also come from Łódź (he was also born here). The brothers Katchalscy vel Katzirowie, one of whom was later a world-renowned scientist and the other president of Israel spent their childhoods there. There is the city's controversial writer Jerzy Kosinski. This is where the Film School is located, which was completed by, among others, Roman Polański. Currently, one of the stars of the NBA is a Łódź-based Marcin Gortat.

Besides, Poland is an extremely grateful area for collectors of historical curiosities.

Often the information about Łódź, where Zishe was allegedly born was then was called a small place, sometimes called the village - "small Eastern provincial town". On the contrary, at that time, Łódź certainly was not; it was one of the most recognizable cities of the then Kingdom of Poland. At the time when Zishe was supposedly born there it had over 200,000 inhabitants! Therefore, even for this reason, he could not be born in Łódź, because it was not a small provincial town or a village, as some people write about the place of his birth. Stryków was, however, such a small provincial town. Very often, people writing the history of his life, and those who do not come from Poland have problems with translating and understanding their names, i.e.: towns or names and the so-called. idioms. Problems are also caused by the intricate and often incomprehensible history of Poland or the neighboring countries.

Extremely interesting information included a short biography of the strongman written by Leon Berg and published in Warsaw in 1925 entitled *Zisza Brajbard, Strongman of the Twentieth Century*. The same book would later be published in the same year in Yiddisch: *The Life Story of the Strongest Man in the World, Zishe Breitbard and His Heroic Feats*. This author, gives the wrong place of his birth, misspells Łódź and 5 Brzezina Street. However, he soon cites the words that Zishe himself had to say, which read:

"When I was 8 years old, together with my grandfather, we went on a trip from Stryków to the village of Dobra to buy a cow. It turned out that we would not be able to transport her back. Therefore, we carried it back. "

This is an unusual quote that tells you directly where the strongman was born and lived in the first years of life. The author quotes after all the words spoken by the strongman!

That's all digressions about Łódź.

Was there any trace left of him in Stryków?

In such situations, it is best to find sources such as the oldest inhabitants of the city. In 1980, the pre-war resident of Stryków, Natan Szafran born there in 1925, would come back every year to spend his holidays from his residence in Las Vegas. In August 2014, when asked about Zishe Breitbart, he replied:

"About Breitbart it was said in Stryków before the war, people knew that he had made a huge career in America. I know that, being a rich man, he sent money to Stryków, which used for the poorest residents as well as for the synagogue in Stryków. When I lived in the USA, I often heard about them, that is, about three brothers, strongmen: Zishe, Gustawa and Józef. The family, however, had to move out of Stryków, because of the Breitbart in my time when I lived in Stryków there was only a family of butchers. It was difficult to receive information from the rest of the world. I do not recall that anyone in Stryków had a radio at that time, and the newspaper literally passed from hand to hand, from home to home. It happened that my father, when he waited his turn, received a newspaper published a week, two weeks, and sometimes a month earlier. So it was difficult to learn more about Breitbart. "

46. Nathan Szafran remembered stories about Breitbart from his childhood

Nathan Szafran raised a very important fact about the life of a strongman. In Germany, he was remembered as a person who helped the poorest people, especially the Jews. It turns out that this help also reached Strykow. It must have been real, because it was preserved in the memory of the locals.

Mr. Szafran died in 2015. During World War II, he was among others a prisoner of concentration camps in Birkenau, Matthausen.

And what happened to the strongman's closest family?

The oldest of the seven siblings is Aron Szlama born in 1890, if based on Zishe's memories, he would be the brother he told the first time that he wanted to be "New Samson" in the future. He rests at the Jewish cemetery in Łódź. Similarly, the father died in 1930 with Icek Hersz and sister Sura (also known as Sonja) and grandfather Gerszon - they are also resting in the Jewish cemetery at Bracka Street in Łódź. The mother was buried in Stryków.

The strongmen's career was successfully followed by brothers Josek (Josef, Józef, Joe) and Gershon (Gustaw, Gustaff). They too were characterized by exceptional strength, although not as such as their brother. Their performances were usually advertised as a show of the strength of the "King Iron" brothers. It also happened that each of them was also given the nickname "King of Iron". However, this was most likely the case as we would say today for purely commercial reasons. The name and title worn by the famous brother was a decoy to attract viewers. Gershon even had a comparison to the "Contemporary Samson," who toured the entire globe, and his performances in Paris, America, Argentina, Brazil, Prague and Warsaw are very popular. " Józef gained enormous popularity in France, he even tried his strength in boxing matches. He became a soldier in the French army and in 1932 he fought two official fights in the professional ring. In France, he was caught up by the outbreak of World War II. He was mobilized to join the French army as a soldier captured, from which he had to escape and join the French resistance movement. After the war, he was awarded the highest French state decorations, he was a French strongman and a *King of Iron*. A photo from 1959 shows him lifting his friends with whom he performed in circus numbers.

47. Gustav Breitbart, brother of Zishe, also attracted huge crowds

93

Gustav, in turn, before World War II, traveled with his own group almost all over the world. He also performed in Poland. A poster announcing his performance in Grajewo has been preserved, for which he was supposed to arrive after an unusual American tour that was extremely popular. Gustaw, Gershon, Gerszon (sometimes called Herman) in 1936-1939 performed with the Magician Kassner. He was one of the assistants of the German illusionist Alois Kassner, famous for the magical shows in Europe. He died in Israel in 1961.

It turns out that Zishe's sister also had above average strength. On Saturday, 26 July 1930, in Lviv, in the Colosseum cinema, there was "one guest performance of the Iron Queen Sonia Breitbart, the sister of the late Zygmunt Breitbart with the participation of J. Breitbart".

The son of Zishe Breitbart, Ossi (Yossi, Oscar) was to die during the Holocaust (shoah). As a child, he was also characterized by extraordinary strength. He won competitions for young strongmen in his youth! Sometimes he performed with his father! Zishe's wife was murdered by the Nazis, shared a similar fate.

About 100 kilometers from Stryków there are towns: Zelów and Szczerców. It was in them that before the Second World War there lived a family named Brajtbart. Some of them survived the nightmare of war, and Mortko Brajtbart went to the USA and wrote down his memoirs as Morris Breitbart: *Awaiting Miracle - the holocaust diaries Morris Breitbart*. It is unusual and at the same time interesting that he changed his name (just like Zishe) and it is still a question of whether these Brajtbarts were relatives of Brajtbart from Stryków. Maybe someday someone will solve this mystery.

What happened to the large estate that belonged to the strongman? The newspapers reported that "he left a huge fortune in both hemispheres."

The villa on the outskirts of Berlin, which was his apartment, is located north of the city center of Oranienburg in the Friedrichsthal district. From the beginning of the 20th century, it became a suburb of the big city of Berlin because it had perfect conditions for it - it is located in a wooded place. No wonder Zishe was looking for happiness and peace there. He lived there until 1924, and in the memory of the inhabitants he signed up as the one who helped the poor. The memory of him is so strong that some say that he was born there! Since February 2013, a street nearby in the villa where he lived received the name Siegmunt Breitbart at the initiative of Klaus Humburg, who admits family ties with Zishe Breitbart. It was he who in 1991 hung the commemorative plaque on the wall of the house once belonging to the Breitbart's. He recalls that Zishe was not only

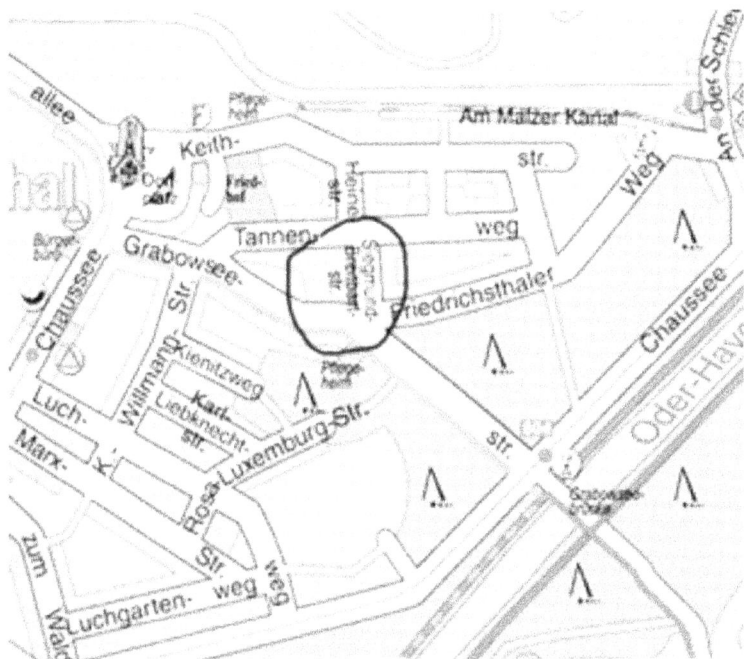

48. Siegmund Breitbart Street in Oranienburg

physically strong, but "he was above all a humble and honest man who helped many Jewish citizens." He is the owner of photos showing the queue of people gathered at the Breitbart villa waiting for a meal.

And that's where Zishe lived to see the street named in his honor!

The street name ceremony was organized in connection with the 120th anniversary of Breitbart's birth. The report from the local press titled: Union of strength and faith. The title is very eloquent and the whole event has an ecumenical character. In the local church on the altar a menorah was set - a symbol of Judaism, Jews, Christians and representatives of other faiths gathered there. An artistic program was prepared to remind people of the unusual character of Zishe - connecting all people regardless of origin, religion and views.

The estate of the strongman was estimated at millions of dollars, but after his tragic death it turned out that almost nothing left him.

How do we know about it? What has become of him?

A few years after the death of the strongman in Berlin, a court trial took place with the participation of Zishe's wife. She was called the Jewish "queen". It turned out that the strongman after his death left his wife only 200 marks, and all his property he had to give to the neediest people.

The documents and certificates submitted at the hearing showed that he distributed his property to various charitable causes without leaving any inheritance. He bestowed hospitals, orphanages, old people's homes and schools. He supported poor Jewish communities, especially in Central and Eastern Europe. He was a philanthropist and what was constantly emphasized during the process to become a model for the young Jewish generation who saw in him a beautiful picture of physical fortitude and a man gushing with health, humor and life optimism. Everywhere he won, gained sympathy for the masses and hearts of Jews. He lived and reciprocated his popularity with philanthropy. He gave his whole heart and with a generous hand helped the poor with special interest caring about physical education of children. For the 200 marks left by him, the wife opened a bar for cabins in the northern district of Berlin. She applied for a license to sell alcohol there. Until she obtained permission, she decided to sell it secretly anyway. Later in the court, she explained that such a pub without alcohol would not be possible. The judge conducting the case, bearing in mind the good done by her husband, punished her with 20 marks. Summing up the whole event in the court hearing, one could read that Breitbart "was a modest and quiet man in private life. Far away from publicity he cared zealously for the family for which he was an exemplary husband and father. Nothing indicated that he was the *King of Iron* when he was observed in the family circle. Throughout his life he broke iron bars, he was breaking chains, he never tried to break off one chain. On the contrary, each link was even stronger. Link of the chain that joined him with the Jewish nation with Jewish destiny. "

Is not this the perfect description of another character - Superman, who will be born more than a dozen years later in the pages of the comic book?

The fact that after many years the figure of a strongman has been recalled is to a large extent the merit of the relative related to strongman Gary Bart. He devoted most of his life to searching for all information about the Brajtbart family - Breitbart. He is one of the few people who can prove his family relationship with a strongman. Apart from him, doctor William Breitbart, born in 1951 in the USA, can prove his family connection with Zishe Beitbart. Apparently, he is family to a strong man. He is considered to be a world-renowned expert in the field of psychosomatic medicine, psycho-oncology and palliative care. This physician, scientist and teacher was born and raised where Zishe also lived, which is on the Lower East Side in Manhattan. His mother emigrated from Turku in Poland to the USA in 1949.

When Zishe's death, another trial began, which continues to this day - basically everyone who bears the name Breitbart considers the strongman as his relative.

The Jewish cemetery in Stryków, where most of the so-called strongman's ancestors are buried was founded in the Eighteenth Century in the north-western part of the city. Its area was about 1.2 hectares. The first serious destruction of the cemetery occurred during World War I, when the Russians dug trenches in its vicinity. The synagogue and cemetery were completely destroyed during World War II. In December 1939, it was burned by the Germans, and less than two years later, also mined and blown up by them. After the war, industrial plants were built on the part of the cemetery, but still in 1946 the last burial took place here.

Today, there are several old, mainly wooden houses in the town that remember the times of the Brajtbart family. On the Evangelical cemetery, there are old, metal-cast iron ornamental fences surrounding the graves - who knows if their father Zishe and maybe even he himself did?

WHERE DID SUPERMAN COME FROM?

In the years 1880-1920, about two million Jews emigrated from Eastern Europe to America. Among them are Mitchell and Sara Siegel, who came to Cleveland from today's Lithuania. From Rotterdam, Juliusz Shuster, emigrated to Toronto and from Kiev to the same city came Ida, who will soon be the wife of Juliusz. To both of the named couple's sons were born in 1914. The Shusters' son is named Joe and Siegel's is Jerry. Both boys meet in 1931 in Cleveland (the Shusters family moves from Canada to this city) at Glenville High School. Both youngsters become close, thanks to common interests. They are passionate about stories from the borderline of fantasy, science, fiction and stories recorded in illustrations or comics. In January 1933, in the pages of their science fiction fanzine, a villain with telepathic abilities appeared.

What inspired Shuster and Siegel?

This story was to be based on the concept of the Superman described by Fryderyk Nietzsche in the book entitled *Thus Spoke Zarathustra*. Inspired by the idea of *Übermensch* (superman) contained in it, Siegel wrote *The Reign of the Superman*. He presented a gentle man transformed into a powerful villain oriented to world domination. Later, however, they decided to make this character a hero. That's how The Superman was created (it was in 1934) and this is the story that will be released in the first issue of Action Comics.

The myth of the superman existed in the imagination of poets and writers.

Bernard Shaw wrote *Man and Superman*. This title, however, did not affect the future creation of Superman, but popularized the term "Superman".

However, a large role in the creation of Superman was played by the fantastic - scientific novel by Philip Wylie from 1930 entitled *Gladiator*. Her main character is endowed with superhuman strength and speed. Another novel by the same author entitled: *When Worlds Collide* took the motive of escape from the planet, which awaits annihilation. In the work of another science fiction writer Edgar Rice Burroughs from the book, *Princess Mars*, there is a story about the adventures of the main character on Mars.

At that time, Dick Tracy appeared another fictitious hero - a detective series of American comics issued since 1931.

Of course, the creators also drew inspiration from Judaism. The idea of the savior of the nation was taken from the biblical Moses (the arrival of Superman to Earth refers to the biblical story of Moses), and the idea of a hero performing acts impossible for an ordinary man from the biblical Samson. There is also the figure of Golem, created in the 16th century by a rabbi from Prague in response to attacks on the Prague Jews. He was to defend them against attackers, he was a creature made of clay in the shape of a man but deprived of soul and speech - as a mindless being he could not be a role model.[18] He was an unpredictable defender of enormous strength, which he could not always control. It was the result of an incomplete experiment. Such a figure had to have a different, more spiritual and naturalistic nature. Incidentally, the rabbi who recorded this was born in Poznan and later settled in Wrocław, so here, too, there is a Polish thread in Superman's history. It should also be added that the history of Golem is really a legend about a rabbi, who thanks to his knowledge of Kabbala, revived a creature made of clay and mud comes from Polish lands, specifically from Chełm. It was recorded by the local rabbi, Eliahu ben Yehuda, called Baal Shem. The whole world, however, knows the later version transferred in space and time to Prague.

Wili Eisner, one of the founders of the American comic book, wrote that Golem was seen as the first Jewish superhero. During the period of mass persecution, the myth about the clay defender of the Jewish minority was especially vivid. Golem himself even got his series of comics published by Marvel entitled Golem - the thing that walks like a man. Despite the fact that no mention was made of Judaism, it was not concealed that the reader had to do with a Jewish hero.

The Kryptonian surname of Superman is Kal - El (Kal - L) which is supposed to resemble the Hebrew "God's voice". The suffix - El comes from the Semitic word for God, it refers to biblical characters whose names end in -el: Isra-el, Dani-el, Samu-el. In turn, the earthly name Kal-Ella-Clark was to be inspired by the name of the American actor Clark Gable, and his name Kent was to come from the name of another actor, Kent Taylor.

18. Arnold Goldsmith, *The Golem Remembered, 1909-1980: Variations of a Jewish Legend* (Wayne State University Press, 1981), p. 22

49. A representation of a Golem

Wili Eisner emphasized that creating superheroes is nothing other than "rebranding" biblical characters. "We are" the People of the Book. " Above all, we are story-tellers. I think that everyone who has come into contact with Jewish culture has possessed the instinct of the story for good, "he said.

Clark Kent, with slick hair in his horny glasses, played the roles of an eternal unlucky man, and slurries of Jewish jokes - shams and tales.

Superman was raised by God-fearing farmers for a good American boy, and he received his super powers as a gift on earth.

The religious Jewish fathers bless their sons on Friday nights to be like Ephraim and Menashe - two sons of Joseph, who grew up to be decent people despite the moral corruption that surrounded them in Egyptian captivity.

Slam Bradley is a fictional character appearing in a series of comics published by DC Comics since 1937. The main character is a private amateur detective who is to help the police in solving difficult cases. He had a bicep and a powerful torso, and he combined strength with intelligence. It was this comic that preceded the release of Superman.

In 1933-37, the school friend of Siegel and Shuster was Tony Strobl. He helped them create the Superman character. He later became a respected artist, especially in Western Europe, illustrating, among other things, Disney's comics.

50. The creators of the comic Superman
Jerry Siegel and Joe Shuster

Siegel and Shuster were interested in film productions in which actors performed dangerous scenes without the intervention of stuntmen and security guards. *Safety Last* from 1923 was one such film. Hard Lloyd, who plays the main role, is an inconspicuous and shy individual, gets into dangerous trouble all the time. The most characteristic scene of the film is the one in which it he hangs from the tall building holding the hands of the clock.

The movie, *The Sign of Zorro* was also important. The role of the title character was played by Douglas Fairbanks, who is a Californian aristocrat wearing a black mask to defend his homeland against the Spanish occupation. He delighted the audience with energy, temperament, audacity and physical fitness. He did the stunt scenes himself. From then on, he played heroes who fought evil.

They also became interested in the almost half-mythical figure of John Henry from the second half of the nineteenth century, who was to be blessed with strength, allowing him to do physical work better than machines.

There was also some influence attributed to Tarzan, who first appeared on the pages of the novel in 1912. Tarzan's cry in the jungle heralded the help of the endangered and annihilation of the sowers of anxiety.

Siegel admitted that "his writing was strongly influenced by the spread of anti-Semitism - he knew and felt that Samson was the model for Superman, who was the answer to Nazism."[19]

It was quite the typical thinking of two young men who, in response to persecution not necessarily related to their origin, and whatever, dreamed of possessing superhuman strength and repaying their oppressors. It should also be remembered that at that time and in the USA, anti-Semitic moods were quite strong. Anti-Jewish rallies were organized, windows in Jewish shops were broken. Universities in the "Ivy League" limited the number of students of Jewish origin. The advertising industry did not employ Jewish artists, just like newspapers printing comic strips. The publishing of comics books with sensational stories, somewhere off the beaten track, belonged to Jewish publishers. Ironically, the word "Superman" can be translated as "übermensch" meaning the key concept of racial philosophy. No wonder that later on the other side of the Atlantic in Europe, and precisely in Germany, this figure provoked the fury of fascist propaganda boss Josef Goebels. He wrote a lot of cruel words against the authors of the comic book. No one understood the power of propaganda and the role of entertainment better than him. The Nazi feared the comic Superman.

Also important was the tragic death of Siegel's father - the righteous man, whom he never spoke about, but that was when he was to think of a flying man or even a superman who would save his life.

For Shuster and Siegel, the impulse to create such a character might have been

19. Jerry Siegel, *The Creation of a Superhero*, unpublished manuscript, 1976, pp. 12-13.

watching Zishe Breitbart's performances during his tour of America in 1923. His life, supernatural feats, worked on the imagination of young Americans.

All these experiences, observations and experiences shaped the type of hero they created. Superman became him.

As a visitor from another planet, he is supposed to be a reflection of a representative of a foreign culture, an immigrant who has acclimated to a new, unknown society. This was an allusion to the creators of Superman, who were also immigrants, but also to Zishe himself. Superman is gifted with superhuman abilities and thanks to that he helps and protects the weaker and oppressed. He wears a blue - red costume with a cape, modeled on a circus strongman's costume. On his chest is a symbol - a large Latin letter S, which is inscribed in a diamond-like shield. The best-known nickname that is given to him is "The Man of Steel", and therefore "Man of Steel" and this is the name that inevitably accompanies all publications about him.

Superman is the most famous illegal immigrant (the Anglo-Saxon term "illegal alien" is in this case extremely adequate), which became the incarnation of everything American. It is an assimilation icon.

In 1935, Joe Shuster, during a holiday at the Green Mansion resort located on a lake in the north of New York, met a man crossing the street. His name was Stanley Weiss, he was 24 years old and he was also a Jewish emigrant from Central and Eastern Europe. He dealt with the sale of furniture on a daily basis. It was at a time when he said "he was thinking of refreshing Superman's physical appearance".

- Can I sketch your face? - asked the surprised passer-by.

After less than a moment he declared triumphantly that

51. Stanley Weiss, the face of Superman

104

he already had the full and complete image of Superman. In the appearance of Stanley Weiss, the face was characterized by a well-defined and protruding jaw. And this characteristic jaw from then until now is also one of the features of Superman's distinctive appearance. Earlier, the jaw of this super hero was also characteristic, but more "sculpted".

Superman had to float and spin easily in the air, so he had to be well built, but also quite tall with a slender figure. The massive silhouette of the strongman was therefore not very suitable for this role.

That is why Shuster was thinking about how to make his appearance look more like a flying bird than an athlete flying when the comic hero was born. It was him who made Superman's figure evolve.

This story is described by Tim Teeman in *The Times* article entitled *"And my father was Superman. Jewish roots comic book hero"* from 2013.02.03. He also adds that "Superman came from the planet Krypton, where his name was Kal - el. This verbal assembly resembles the Hebrew word for God's voice. His physical appearance and posture resembled an American Jew, a circus performer of Polish descent, Siegmund Breitbart, and such figures as Samson or the mythical Golem."

Weiss helped to complement these characteristics.

Siegel in turn invented the face of Superman - a face understood as a personality. "Superman can have a double identity. It can be quiet and gentle, but it will also have a crazy character and will do all sorts of wonderful things. "

Every day, Superman is a calm and shy newspaper employee, and this thread came from Shuster himself, who for some time worked for the *Toronto Star* newspaper. Lois Lane was modeled on Siegel's great love, his wife Joanne.

Siegel and Shuster created their comic not only on paper, which they often missed, but also on cardboard cartons. When it was made, it was still necessary to sell it, and the attempts made for this purpose lasted several years. They believed that it would be the work of their lives, which would radically change their fate. Finally, he found the coveted publisher and offered a fee of $130. Even for those times it was a small sum, but it pleased them - they were happy that anyone wanted to take on the comic. It is not known whether in a fit of happiness or lack of experience, by signing the contract, they neglected one very important detail - the contract deprived them of copyright to the created characters.

The comic made its debut on June 1, 1938, and it was a time of dark persecution of Nazi Germany. He gained recognition among readers almost overnight. In the 1940s, annual pay for comic artists totaled $ 7,500. With the millions of profits taken by the publishing house, it was a ridiculous amount. Since 1947, in which desperate artists have begun a court battle with the publishing house, a dispute over due royalties continues to this day. The heirs of Siegel and Shuster continue this.

From the time when the publishing house took the form of the original authors and handed them over to other cartoonists and scriptwriters, no longer necessarily with Jewish roots, Superman became a more Greek hero of the messianic character. This is particularly evident in the movie about Superman where Marlon Brando is depicted as a God who sends his son among mortals. In the same vein, subsequent artists modified his physical appearance, referring clearly to the Greek antiquity.

In principle, all the most important creators of the so-called The Golden and the Silver Age of the comic book were born in the families of Jewish immigrants from Eastern Europe. The characters created by them to a greater or lesser extent were equipped with certain features, emotions or references to Jewish history or culture. Virtually none of them came from an orthodox religious family (they were not experts on the Torah, Mishnah, Talmud or Kabbalah), but they all grew up in a Jewish environment, they had Bar - Mitzvah, they listened to Haggadah or midrash to children told instead of various fairy tales. It is certain, however, that the culture in which they grew up had an impact on their work. They created characters and provided them with a set of features and behaviors guided by their vision of the world. They did not act, of course, only within a certain group of people, but they addressed their work to a mass audience and matched it to his liking. They were artists of Jewish descent that were more likely to be included in the trend of "Think Yiddish, act British", that is, creating in Yiddish, but also for non-Jewish audiences. Superheroes are a combination of the Greek cult of beauty and physicality with the ethics and philosophy of Judaism.

It was from Superman that the greatest popularity of comic books began, and thanks to this character, comics got from newspaper stores to the world of cultural anthropologists. This character gave rise to other heroes of pop culture. In the late seventies of the twentieth century, the state university in Indiana announced that anyone who will present an interesting project will be able to lead a lecture for students. One of the volunteers was Michael Uslan, who proposed a lecture on comics. The dean politely refused to take a series of lectures on "funny pictures"

106

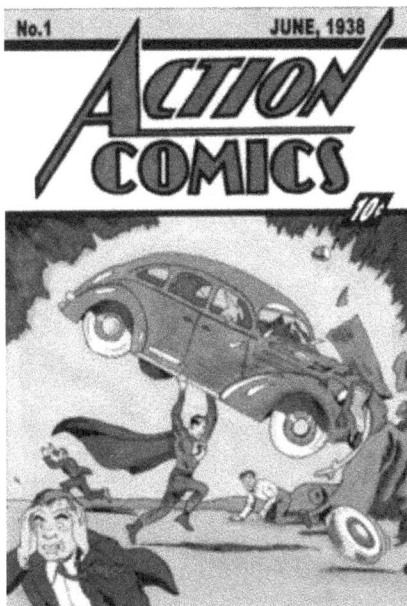

52. The first comic featuring Superman

as a variant of 20th century mythology and contemporary folklore. Uslan did not give up and took the dean to summarize the story of Moses. When he reluctantly did this, he was asked to accurately sum up Superman's story. The dean, after a few sentences, stopped his lecture and accepted the project presented to him. Uslan later became a producer of cinema adaptations of "Batman".

Superman seems to be unquestionably the icon of the number one of world pop culture. He gave birth to many other heroes created in his likeness. Today Superman is a brand that brings gigantic profits. A thirty-page comic when it hit the market cost just 10 cents. In recent years, he has gained dizzying prices - one of the surviving copies found the buyer for USD 2.16 million, which made him the most expensive comic book in the world. The original bill for the said $130 which the comic writers collected in 1938 on the online auction was sold for $160,000. In 2010, a copy of the comic in which Superman appeared - Action Comics No.1 from June 1938 was sold for a million dollars at an online auction organized by one of the New York websites.

KAROL   KRAUSER   (PIWOWORCZYK)   -
FORGOTTEN SUPERMAN.

Who was the first movie Superman?

None of the American cinema stars seemed to be like that today.

Today, an almost unknown the person who first lent his image to advertisements for the animated movie of Superman's adventures is of Polish origin, Karol Karol Krauser's, actually Karol Piwoworczyk. He was born in 1912 in Hollyoke, a city in the state of Massachusetts, which has a concentration of emigrants from Poland (currently ¼ of its inhabitants identify their roots in Poland). Krauser was first a Polish wrestler (competing, among others, in 1939 in New York), and then a wrestler appearing in the Russian group of Kalmikoffs brothers. He also worked as a model at Fleischer Studios. It was thanks to this that his silhouette appeared in the first animated film in 1941 telling the story of Superman's adventures. What is important is the silhouette, Krauser's body structure is very similar to Zishe Breitbart's figure. The nickname "Polish Apollo" stuck to him, and photographs of his likeness were signed like that. Zishe was also called that, and the similarity of both men is quite striking. It is probably no coincidence that a wrestler of Polish origin was hired for this role.

53. Karol Krauser (on the left) with other Polish wrestlers in New York, 1939

108

Karol Krauser
Model for the
Super man cartoon
at the
Fleischer Studios
Miami - Fla.

54. Karol Krauser in the Superman costume

THE YEAR 1991 BREITBART IS BACK, AS A COMIC BOOK, SUPERMAN RETURNS TO EUROPE

Despite the fact that Zishe gave birth to the icon of pop culture, his character was almost forgotten for years. You can learn more about why this was in part from the publication *Men of Tomorrow: Geeks, Gangsters, and the Birth of the Comic Book* by Gerard Jones. The main thesis is the disputes of the publishing house with the authors of the comic forced some of the ideas and characters had to disappear from the content of the Superman comic.

There is an interesting very old illustration from the collection of Gary Bart. It shows Breitbart performing in the circus and is clearly associated with "colorful pictures", which is related to the genre of pictorial history that we now call a comic book! Who knows if this illustration was not a huge impulse for creating a comic Superman?!

One the cover of the first issue of the Superman comic the main character is holding a car with a raised hand. It is associated with similar illustrations - Breitbart's posters, encouraging people to watch his performances. The first page of the comic book and what Superman can do, what he is famous for is nothing more than references to Breitbart's life. We learn that Superman has been was admired for his extraordinary strength since he was a child: he broke chains, he was able to stop a locomotive, railway rails were bent over his head. In this case, some of these comic images are almost identical to the strongman's photographs used during his performances. Yet another fragment of this comic book below an illustration of the title character tells the reader that:

"SUPERMAN! This is the Champion in rescuing people from oppression. Admired for his personality, which is completely dedicated to saving people in need of help!" This is nothing more than Breitbart's motto.

The seventeenth issue of the comic book about the adventures of Superman from 1939 is shows the main character crushing Adolf Hitler in the hand on the cover. Superman fights fascism. This is probably a reference to Zishe Breitbart's story.

However, it was not until April 1991 that DC COMICS INC released comic strip No. 54 from the *Superman* series consisting of: *Lost in the 1940s and The Warsaw Ghetto*. Its authors are: Jerry Ordway, Dennis Janke, Karl Kesel.

Superman is moved in time and wakes up in the circus. It is 1943. He immediately remembers his earthly incarnation when he was a circus performer. He learns that there is a war and he gets a job in a circus. He performs the same spectacular numbers again that took place when he was still in the earthly incarnation as Zishe Breitbart. He charms everyone with extraordinary strength, and his performance begins by calling him Samson. He rips metal chains, raises elephants or drives onto the stage with a chariot drawn by horses. It arouses widespread admiration and disbelief that his skills are real. He travels with the circus all over America, visits the cities of Chicago, Cincinnati, Philadelphia, and all performances are called as the arrival of Samson - the Man of Steel. The comic tells that this is the beginning of his great future, immortal fame and career. At some point Spectrum, which manages his fate, sends him where he is most needed. In June 1943 Superman goes to Poland in the Warsaw ghetto. On the spot he sees the terrible fate of the Jewish population and declares war on the Third Reich. He also wants to save the remaining Jews who survived the liquidation of the Jewish quarter in Warsaw. It was liquidated in mid-May 1943. SS units were still tracking those who survived, and the distraught Superman asks himself that if he had arrived here earlier he could change the "timeline of history" or change the sequence of historical events. He stops the train with people destined for extermination, deported to concentration camps. This is done in such a way that it destroys the locomotive running on it. People are escaping from the wagons and they are grateful to him. The Nazis, seeing this extraordinarily strong man, commented that "this man could do more harm to the Reich than all Stalin's armies." He kills the perpetrators, and his most important goal is to prevent the Nazi missile produced with an atomic bomb that can kill the world. "I have to take this deadly scrap ... up ... high ... high where it does not hurt anyone" - it's his answer to the information that the Germans launched its deadly weapons. He flies into space to meet it with extraordinary strength that allows him to intercept it and fly with it to heaven. At some point, the people watching him are lost, and after a while they see a huge explosion. The Nazis are disconsolate and cannot believe that "he destroyed everything in a few minutes, what we did over the years!" Superman dissolved with the atomic bomb, saving humanity. Happy Jews are happy that their "angel has found his way to heaven, but first he gave them freedom."

This is the part of this comic that refers to the life of Zishe Breitbart.

2001 - Breitbart as "Invincible"

The memory of Zishe Breitbitt returned at the beginning of the 21st Century all thanks to the German director Werner Herzog. In 2001, the production of *Invincible* hit the movie screens. The film, based partly on real events, tells the story of a Jewish strongman who becomes a symbol of Germany's strength. The strongman is Zishe.

Why did Herzog get interested in him?

The director, as he says about his work, has always been interested in people who are a bit different from social norms - enthusiasts, visionaries whose lives are determined by overarching ideas. He became a strongman born in Stryków thanks to Gary Bart - a descendant of a strongman, also a film producer. "He had a lot of material from his ancestor and thank God, the nerve to let me in" - so the director talked about the producer of the film. It is Bart, (his name in the film production is Jan) who almost all his life devoted to collecting all information about the strongman was the main person who inspired the creation of the film. For the purposes of the scenario, Zishe's birth certificate was aged by ten years, thus reproducing the error concerning Breitbart's birth that appeared in his lifetime. The fact that the film Zishe is born in Galicia, then belonging to the Austro-Hungarian Empire is also an invention of a film scenario.

What purpose did the authors have in making the film?

It was most likely to show growing anti-Semitism, especially in that region, in those times. From there, anti-Semitism moved to Vienna or Berlin. In the film scenario, Zishe warns mankind against fascism, which has just been strengthening in Germany. The entire screenplay is a confusion of life facts with the fiction of Zishe Breitbart, and therefore cannot be considered as his film biography.

55. Scene from the movie The Invincible. Zishe's father was Gary Bart, who was related to Breitbart

Historical figures appear in the film, such as Hermann Göring, a fascist politician or Erik Jan Hanussen, with whom Zishe has been involved in the aforementioned dispute.

The film's action is shifted by ten years from the actual events, that is, from the times when Zishe was in Vienna or Berlin and had contact with Hanussen. This is purposeful, it was about showing the growing threat of fascism.

The role of Zishe Breitbart is played by authentic Finnish strongman Jouko Ahola, twice the winner of the title of the strongest man in the world, he is partnered by British actor Tim Roth, as Hanussen and Anna Gourari, as a film pianist Marta Farra, the beloved of Zishe.

In the screenplay, Zishe comes from eastern Poland from the town of Elza, located near the town of Kielce. Elza is a fictitious city that never exists while Kielce is located about 150 km from Stryków, the place where Zishe Breitbart was born and lived. When Poland was annexed, this area (film Kielce and its surroundings) belonged to the Austro-Hungarian Empire to the province of Galicia.

The film's action begins at the beginning of the 1930s in Eastern Poland, which is now independent. Zishe gets provoked into a fight by anti-Semitic doctrines. To pay for the damages he takes up work in the circus, where he defeats of an inveterate strongman without any effort. Erik Jan Hanussen, an associate of the fight in the arena, is convincing Breitbart that a great future awaits him in Berlin.

Zishe sets out for Germany and goes to the occult palace run by Hanussen. The Germans are the time when Nazis from NSDAP, who are frequent visitors to the occult palace, are coming to power. Zishe is disguised as an Aryan, gets a blond wig and a Nordic helmet performing on stage as the strongest man in the world, Siegfried. This name is of Germanic origin, a hero from Norse mythology derived from the words victory and care and is the one who provides security to his followers. Siegfried, in whose role he played Zishe, becomes a symbol of Germany's strength. He consciously created himself as a noble soldier using the symbolism of German nationalism (the already mentioned blond hair, blue eyes, the name Siegfried - typically Nordic characters). This is to help him gain popularity. It all lasts until one of Breitbart's performances unexpectedly dumps the disguise, announcing to the German audience that he is a Jew. This happens under the influence of the younger brother who persuaded him to do so. It is to be a symbolic transformation of this character.

The film is about the real conflict between Breitbart and Hanussen, but its background is a bit different than it was in reality. The situation is similar with the film were Zishe loved Marta Farra, which in turn in authentic relations was supposed to be a counterbalance to his strength.

This time Zishe accuses Hanussen of using fraudulent practices in screenings. During the court trial, it turns out that Hanussen is not, as he himself claimed, a Danish nobleman, but Jewish-Czech. SA Bojówki arrest Hanussen, and his body is found after eleven days in the woods near Berlin. These two facts presented in the film are consistent with the historical truth.

Under the influence of the events he experienced, Zishe undergoes a kind of internal transformation. He is religious and believes that he has found his true calling. He sees himself as the "New Samson," who must save his people from the impending doom. Again, he returns to eastern Poland on foot, warning every one of the fascist threat. He damages his knee in the course of his mission. Undeterred by this, he continues his march. When he finally goes to the hospital, it's too late. Within three weeks he is subjected to eleven operations. However, they fail to save his life and dies two days before Hitler comes to power.

The further authentic fate of Hanussen is equally intriguing. He was called the seer of Adolf Hitler; he had predicted Hitler's rise to power, thirty days before the event, or the burning of the Reichstag. In Berlin, he led a famous occult palace, in which he foretold the future, and his clients were the elite of Germany at that time.

On 1 January 1935, he solemnly handed Adolf Hitler an amulet, the mandrake root dug out at Hitler's birthplace, depicting the figure of a man who was to ensure his success. The event was recorded by the Viennese press, and Hanussen stated that the chief can never part with this talisman, otherwise he will be lucky. Hitler and his entourage celebrated the effective power of amulets and talismans. The mandrake root kept by Hitler at the Orle Gniazdo mansion in Bavaria was stolen, which he was supposed to react to by a fury attack. Hanussen gave the leader advice and advice in the field of psychology.

Hanussen knew the story behind various events and was uncomfortable for some of the personalities. He was sued for extortion, but the court acquitted him when during the trial he specified ... the amount and type of money in the pockets of the judges and the prosecutor.

He was killed along with nearly two hundred personal group of people uncomfortable for the fascist dictatorship during the "night of long knives". Hanussen knew too much about fascist dignitaries, and Hitler himself could not have imagined that there might be a person in his circle who could influence his future.

56. The book, Muscular Power, which Zishe Breitbart co-wrote

The memory of Zishe was revived with the Herzog film. He became a hero of dozens of articles, but also book publications, aimed at children, practicing bodybuilding and strength sports, and on popular-scientific publications. It has been repeatedly continued in English, French and German, a program for beginner bodybuilders and weight lifters, of which he was a co-author: *Power Muscle*. It is also published, slightly changed as the *Strength Training and Physical Culture System*.

Today his origin is defined differently. Of course, it is always a statement that he came from Poland. Sometimes he is a Polish circus artist of Jewish descent, sometimes American, and sometimes German. In the guidebook for young *Power Muscle* strongmen (in addition to the advice for young strongmen, we find newspaper clippings from several American newspapers, in which the term Polish strongman, Polish Hercules appears.

IS IT POSSIBLE TO SPEAK OF SUPERMAN'S CURSE THAT BEGAN WITH ZISHE BREITBART?

It is widely believed that the problems with Superman began from the moment of his comic birth. Shuster and Siegel in connection with the conflict with the publishing house DC Comics, (the legal battle for due royalties lasts until today!) In a fit of anger, they cursed every success regarding the hero they invented.

But did the Superman's curse really start with them?

The first unlucky person was the real "Superman of the Ages" Zishe Breitbart - Superman, who really existed. It is difficult to speak of bad luck in the event of his death. However, this was only the beginning of a black series of strange things that were playing the character of Superman or closely cooperating with him. The last days of the life of Karol Krauser and Stanley Weiss were a band of suffering.

Krauser was struggling with injuries acquired during his athletic career, and Weiss died of an incurable heart defect right before the premiere of Superman in 1978. David, son of Stanley, mentions that the last years of his father's death, aged 57, were one great torment.

57. Kirk Alyn

119

58. George Reeves

Kirk Alyn, the first who appeared in the role of Superman in the film set shortly after the Second World War, became so identified in this role that he was not offered another film contract! Before almost complete financial bankruptcy, despite the success he enjoyed, he wrote an autobiography of how he played the role of Superman. In the 1950s, George Reeves was another star as the serial steel man appearing in *Adventures of Superman*. He died mysteriously three days before his marriage. He supposedly committed suicide, but on the pistol, from which he shot himself, the actor's fingerprints were not found. The TV star had an affair with the wife of one of the film directors. A lover or another woman engaged to him could have killed him.

Another movie Superman did not get better either. Bud Collyer, the superhero's voice in animated TV series and radio programs, died of cardiovascular problems three years after the implementation of *The New Adventures of Superman*. At a very young age, Lee Quigley, the movie Superman - an infant in the production of Richard Donner in 1978, died. The cause of death was ... a drunk.

The most famous is the case of Christopher Reeve, who played the role of Superman four times. Each of the film productions in which the record of popularity took place. However, he did not miss his luck. In 1995, practicing in a horse-riding center, his horse slowed sharply before one of the obstacles, dropping him from the saddle. Although the actor was protected by a helmet but falling to the ground he suffered a lot of damage. The fractured cervical spine caused permanent paralysis from the neck down. The actor miraculously escaped death, but for the rest of his life he had to move around in a wheelchair and breathe with a respirator. He died nine years later due to cardiac arrest caused by antibiotic, anti-sepsis. Sepsis was created as a result of non-healing pressure ulcers and urinary complications (sepsis was also the official cause of Zishe Breitbart's death). It is also interesting that two years after his death, the wife of the movie Superman died from cigarettes and died of lung cancer. However, just before the fatal fall of a horse, American television broadcast the thriller *Above Suspicion*, in which Reeve played ... a paralyzed policeman. This

59. Christopher Reeve

very popular production from 1978 was also extremely tragic. Margot Kidder, the movie Lois Lane, or a beloved hero from the planet Krypton, who performed together with Reeve, underwent a nervous breakdown. She was diagnosed with manic-depressive illness.

The curse was also supposed to reach the crew working on the movie *Superman: Returns*, and specifically on its release in the DVD version. One of its members was robbed and beaten, the second fell from the stairs, and another flew through the glass. The comedian Richard Pryor, appearing in *Superman III*, soon became ill with multiple sclerosis after the film's release. Lane Smith, the editor-in-chief of *The New Adventures of Superman*, died of amyotrophic lateral sclerosis - an extremely rare disease. After playing the role of Superman's biological father in 1978, Marlon Brando received enormous financial success, but experienced a family tragedy. A dozen years later his eldest son killed his half-sister's lover, for which he was sentenced to 10 years in prison.

In the same year in which Reeve had a serious accident, in 1995, the daughter of Marlon Brando, who suffered from depression, committed suicide.

"Superman's curse" is treated by some as an explanation of their failure and at the same time as self-promotion. After the performance in *Superman: Returns* Kate Bosworth received a nomination for Golden Raspberry and blamed the failure of the creation and parting with his beloved man fell on the fate of this production. The actor in the same film, Brendan Routh, says he does not believe in any curses, and so far no unpleasant events have happened to him. They met Ilya Suskind, the producer of iconic films about Superman. He was missing in Mexico at the end of January 2011. He was found a few days later at a local hospital, where he was under the influence of sedatives. As for now, he is the last victim of the Superman's curse. Who will be next? Is the curse or anyone who prefers bad luck, which was born when Breitbart's death continues?

WHY CAN ZISHE BREITBART BE CONSIDERED THE PROGENITOR OF SUPERMAN?

Most of the superheroes had some imaginary genesis. Is it an off-planetary origin, a radioactive accident or a mad scientist's invention? It was not easy for originality. You can see it in the form of Superman, who had his earthly incarnation.

Superman was created as a result of merging into one few figures and historical and semi-legendary events.

The fact that the main inspiration during the creation of the Superman character was the life of the Stryków strongman, among others following facts:

- he was called the Iron King, this nickname was then used to create a Man of Steel
- his performances were promised especially in the USA and Canada, as Superman Centuries shows
- he was the first man to be first identified and later called Superman
- he wore a cape
- advertised on posters as a man able to stop a speeding locomotive
- for example, a car passed through his muscular body during the performance. The film Superman also stretched his muscular body like a string to fill up the missing rail on which a super-express traveled
- it was written about him as "a superman with perfect physical fitness"
- the creators of the Superman character - Siegel and Shuster, being little boys, watched his performances, which, as they emphasized, made a great impression on them
- In creating Superman, the developers drew inspiration from the biblical Samson, the same as Zishe Breitbart was called, the New Samson

You can also find other connections.

Clark Kent, the earthly embodiment of Superman, was a shy and sensitive reporter working in a newspaper every day - just like Breitbart with a gentle disposition.

There is a noticeable similarity between Karol Krauser and actor George Reeves who portrayed Superman to Zishe Breitbart.

Superman flies over the skyscrapers of New York, above the city where the strongman was called Superman of the Ages.

In 1996, Jules Feiffer, a cartoonist and expert in pictorial stories, wrote that the hero of the comic Superman is an "American dream of young Jews" adding that "he arrived not from the fictitious planet Krypton, but from Minsk, Vilnius, Warsaw maybe from Łódź, or Cracow, maybe". Larry Tye, the author of the book *Superman*, wrote in *The Miami Herald* that "Superman came from the planet Poland, maybe from Łódź or Cracow".[20] In another article published in *The Jewish Daily Forward*, he wrote explicitly that Superman is none other than Zishe Breitbart.

Emphasizing features such as a strong will that is capable of realizing impossible stories, it creates Zishe's life as a hero like Nietzsche's superman.

The figure of an invincible man was needed by the Jewish community that met with reluctance caused by prejudices and the threat of national socialism. Zishe Breitbart was such a man for Jews.

The theme of Superman's story is also the phrase that "Great power means great responsibility." Similar, to Brietbart's phrase.

It is Professor Gillerman who studies the history of the Jews and writes that he was an archetype of a muscular man, both a gladiator and a cowboy. He also performed in the "revealing Tarzan's costume".[21]

Zishe, as in the *Superman* comic, wants to fix the world.

---

20. Tye Larry, *Superman*, (University of Nebraska, U.S., Lincoln 2013), p.100
21. Sharon Gillerman, *Strongman Siegmund Breitbart and Interpretations of the Jewish Body, in Michael Brenner and Gideon Reuveni, Emancipation Through Muscles: Jews and Sports in Europe* (Lincoln: University of Nebraska Press, 2006), p. 63.

Like other "Jewish ancestors" - Samson, Superman had his weak point, a mineral called Kryptonite, which deprived him of his superhuman powers. Zishe Breitbart should also be added to this group. In the case of Samson, it was hair, and Breitbart's knee.

Superman brought three determinants to the comic: special powers, double identity and costume. Double identity is an inseparable part of Jewish culture. It is common to have a Hebrew and "ordinary" name for use with the non-Jewish world and, as often happened, completely hide their origin and attempt to "melt" into a certain group and assimilation. The hero called Superman hid under a non-Jewish name, Clark Kent.

Was Zishe Breitbart's character almost identical?

Rabbi Simcha Weinstein finds Superman's tropes on the Pirkei Awot treatise (Sentences of the Fathers). It says that the world is based on three things: truth, justice and peace. Superman's figure fought for truth, justice, but also for the "American way." In yet another passage, the treaty declares that a man should try to be "quick as a leopard, light as an eagle, he is as strong as a deer and strong like a lion". Superman's famous slogan "faster than a bullet, stronger than a locomotive, capable of jumping over the tallest building" seems to be a sort of modern reflection of this sentence and an obvious reference to slogans encouraging to watch performances ... Zishe Breitbart.

In this treatise, we find another motif that interests us: "If there is no leader, try to be a leader."

It means that the one who wants to stand up for others works in a world full of chaos where the law is not enough to defend peace.

Arie Kaplan, the creator of comics in the From Krakow to Krypton, suggests where Comic-book Superman came from.

And finally: What is actually Superman? He is noble, morally impeccable, wise - his judgments are always accurate. For this he is tough, tenacious towards evil and most importantly, all-powerful. It's actually not someone anymore. This is something extraordinary. Nothing more than a phenomenon like Breitbart.

And there is something else.

Today it may seem unlikely, but initially, Superman could not fly! The religious theme, the almost half-American concept of Superman's creation is extremely important. Remember, however, that the same demigod almost accompanied

Zishe Breitbart. One might also wonder if, like the story of Superman and his exodus from a dying planet, it is not very similar to Breitbart's life. He also wants to use his almost limitless powers to become the defender of the oppressed. In other words, this vanishing planet is the world of Jews threatened with persecution and the holocaust. Breitbart's life is indispensable in the context of the whole story of the comic book about Superman. It's an archetype of a super hero and it's not anachronistic at all. Bar-Kochba is in Aramaic, the Son of the Star - it was connected with Breitbart, and Superman also came from among the stars.

This is the end of this extraordinary story. However, it may be the beginning of another story also about Zishe Brietbart, but this time transferred to a comic story and film tape - well, that's because almost everyone has heard about Superman, it's time to get to know his real life ...I hope this book will be such a beginning.

CHRONOLOGY

22 February 1893 - he is born in Stryków

1896/97 - he is convinced of his extraordinary strength and helps his father at work in the forge

1906 - 1908 - joins a Jewish artistic group performing in Stryków, with which he travels across Polish territories - he performs in circuses, is famous for his teeth chewing and breaking up iron chains and breaking up stone blocks on his own chest

1914 - as a subject of the Tsar he is mobilized to the army, he takes part in military operations on the front of the great world war, which breaks out on August 1

Around 1916 - he was taken prisoner by the Germans in Prussia (currently it is a region of Poland beautifully situated on the lakes called - Masuria).

1918 - after the end of World War, he emigrated briefly to the USA, then, after returning to Europe, he makes a decision to stay in Germany, stays on the shows he gave at fairs and streets, marries Emilie Ester Weitz,

1919 - director of Circus Busch offers him a job, he soon starts working under the pseudonym King of Iron with a specially prepared artistic program

1920 - 1922 - tour of Europe, during which he performs in the most important cities and gains the 1922/23 - a series of performances in Vienna, during which he is announced as "New Samson", is a hero of a loud conflict with occultist Jan Erik Hanussen

1923/24 - a series of performances in America, which was advocated as the arrival of the "Superman of the Ages", becomes a US citizen, in New York begins to publish a correspondence course of physical gymnastics enjoying great popularity, is a "builder of strength and health" - it is simply called SUPERMAN

1925 - returns to Europe, performances in Poland, preparation for departure to Palestine, in late July, an unfortunate accident in a circus in Radom while performing one of the standard numbers

12 October 1925 - dies in Berlin due to an infection that entered the body, amputation of both legs and ten operations performed proved ineffective

But it was only the end of earthly life ...

1928 - the writer Jecheskiel Mosze Neumann (Najman) published a fantasy film scenario entitled *The Life of Zishe Breitbart* in the *Film Velt Daily*. The script was written in Warsaw three years after the death of the strongman. Zishe meets Samson in him, who considers him with his twenty-century incarnation.

1938 - *Action Comics* publishes the first issue of the comic book about Superman. The cover shows the main character lifting the car up - it looks almost the same as the posters depicting Zishe Breitbart. The first page of the comic is a reference to the life of a strongman. A year later, the number 17 of this series presents Superman who destroys fascists. Breitbart also fought fascism, and after his death it was people who adhered to this ideology who murdered the closest strongman's family.

1941 - the first adaptation of Superman's adventures on a film tape appears, it is an animated film. The posters advertising this production include the figure of the Polish wrestler Karol Krauser (Piwoworczyk) who appears in the costume of Superman. He was called "Polish Apollo" like Zishe Breitbart. With the reputation of the "Jewish Superman", he buys a villa on the outskirts of Berlin

1991 - CD Comics publishes comic book No. 54 from the Superman series, referring to the life of Zishe Breitbart. Its authors are: Jerry Ordway, Dennis Janke, Karl Kesel.

2001 - A feature film directed by Werner Herzog, entitled *Invincible* based on the life of a strongman, hits the screen.

2014 - the author of this book, Jacek Perzyński, is a director and scriptwriter of a documentary produced by Polish television: *Superman the man from Stryków*. He is the main narrator in it, and the film is about the life of a strongman. There are, among others, rabbi Shalom Ben Stambler, who sings a song about Zishe. The film produced in 2014 was broadcasted on Polish television several times.

PRESS CLIPPINGS

Siegmund Breitbart
A Box Office Record Breaker

By Dave Webster

"Breitbart is the big thrill with his feats of strength and I like the kindly manner and the dignity of the elderly gentlemen who makes his announcements. When he asked someone in the audience to select the side of the chain Breitbart should break, I yelled out 'left' and then Breitbart gave me a piece of the chain for luck! I felt like a star in the show.

"His new motordrome stunt is a wow! Holds the whole dome on his chest while two men on motorcycles rush around it. He's some boy."

The New York Telegraph reported that the Polish strongman with the power of a locomotive broke the house record at the Orpheum Theatre and became the idol of Brooklyn youth and athletic club members who attended en masse.

The regular fans liked Breitbart from the first, for instead of weightlifting, he did novel and sensational stunts with great skill and showmanship. Breitbart is a better showman than Sandow and furthermore he has a greater and more interesting repertoire of stunts."

Amongst his many feats was cutting half inch thick iron bars around his arm. He took a bar 7' long, 1¾" wide and ¼" thick, then bent it to the shape of a three leafed clover. Few could bend bars or break chins like Siegmund could. He bent a 15" x ⅜" square bar into the shape of a horse-shoe and snapped chains with his hands or by expanding his chest but his piece de resistance was the biting through of chains or metal by the strength of his teeth and the power of his jaws.

As THE STEAMSHIP ALBERT BALLIN ARRIVED FROM EUROPE ON AUGUST 26, 1923, A GROUP OF BROAD-SHOULDERED, MUSCULAR MEN GROUPED EXCITEDLY ON THE NEW YORK DOCKSIDE AND THE KNOWLEDGEABLE OBSERVER WOULD HAVE RECOGNIZED AMONGST THEM WLADEK AND STANISLAUS ZBYSKO, THE WORLD CHAMPION WRESTLERS. A WELL DRESSED MAN, WHO APART FROM A THICK, COLUMN-LIKE NECK, LOOKED LIKE A COLLEGE BOY, WALKED DOWN THE GANGPLANK AND THE MUSCLEMEN REACHED TO GRASP HIS HAND: ANOTHER GREAT POLISH STRONGMAN HAD REACHED THE NEW WORLD.

"The Greatest Ever Paid to Strength." This was the description given to the box office successes of Siegmund Breitbart, one of the few European strongmen to capture the hearts of Americans during the 1920's. At that time unparalleled scenes attended his performances in the United States and in Europe as he amazed and dominated theatre audiences, the press and the public.

He had an eight week continuous run at the New York Hippodrome, said to be the largest and finest vaudeville house in the world at that time, playing to more than 65,000 people during Christmas week of 1923. He then did a 40 week tour on the B.F. Keith circuit as the Super-Headline feature, breaking all attendance records. The "Standing Room Only" and "House Full" signs were daily occurrences wherever he appeared. He was said to be earning $7,000 a week at that time, a fantastic amount for such a performer, considering I have records indicating that another strongman of the same period was getting $50 a week for his act.

Typical of the press notices was this extract from the columns of the New York Evening Journal. "Breitbart can roll a railroad tie like a cigarette paper and lays back on a board full of sharp spikes and lets a parade of flattened march across his chest. An electric iron is like a bon bon to that baby and he bites through an iron chain like it was a lump of sugar.

He usually included this as part of his act but although there was public acceptance that this was a genuine feat, strength authorities were most dubious about this being done without trickery. To overcome such scepticism, the strongman would have dentists and surgeons examine his performances and examine his mouth for an official aids. He had many written statements from such professional men declaring that they had found his act to be perfectly genuine. Finally, to put an end to the speculation that they may be special chains or doctored metal, he went to the famous Krupp Steel Works in Essen, Germany and

The photo below shows a picture of the chain that Breitbart was supposed to have bitten through. It is certainly in two pieces and since his biting was carefully observed, apparently he did bite the chain in two. We advise readers not to try anything like this. Teeth are hard to come by and you are sure to break them off if you try this.

In the photo below we see Breitbart biting a chain in two. This is quite a feat in case you have never tried it. It is hard as well. We don't know how these fellows did it or anything about it but the fact that they did it proved that they could do it.

The above photo is of Siegmund Breitbart who was very famous in his time.

60. Breitbart in America -1

Breitbart, Modern Samson
First American Appearance of Jewish Superman

IT seems an anomaly to have a Jew hailed the strongest man in the world. But that is what they say of Sigmund Breitbart, regarded as the superman of physical prowess and perfection. Echoes of the remarkable feats of strength exhibited by this modern Samson have reached us from time to time and of his successful appearances in the theatres of Vienna, London and other European capitals. Recently he made his debut at the Orpheum Theatre in Brooklyn; thence he will travel over the Keith Circuit, appearing at the Palace Theatre in New York during the week commencing December 3.

The youngest son of a mighty blacksmith in the little Polish village where he was born, Breitbart exhibited remarkable power even as a child. His only toys were the horseshoes and nails around his father's shop. While he never had occasion to tear a lion's mouth apart or carry

SIGMUND BREITBART

off the gates of Gaza like Samson of old, or strangle a huge serpent with his hands as Hercules did, there is no telling what Sigmund Breitbart might do in an emergency. Today he can twist an iron bar, snap a steel beam or bite in two a thick metal chain as easily as the average man

can break a match or bite an apple. Moreover, he can put a piece of leather in his mouth, hitch himself to a truck loaded with people and draw it casually around the block.

BREITBART has many pseudonyms. He is known as the Iron King, the Polish Apollo, the Modern Samson, the Superman of Strength. But the remarkable thing about Breitbart is that there is little in his general appearance to indicate the possession of such prodigious strength. True, he is tall and fairly heavy, but his face is that of a thinking human being, unlike one who lives by brute strength alone. He looks like the average well-set athletic young man. In general appearance he somewhat resembles Valentino, the idol of the screen, or perhaps Houdini, the Jewish handcuff king.

Breitbart's hobby is a library of some two thousand volumes on the history of the Golden Age in Rome. Referring to the Roman Coliseum, which he considers the favorite spot in all the world, Breitbart told the interviewer: "I'd take a furnished room there any time. When I was a little boy working in my father's blacksmith shop in Lodz, Poland, I used to love to read about the Roman emperors and generals, and the things they did. I was especially interested in the tortures they tried on people. I would try to devise the same instruments and try them on myself, and most of the time I could stand them without much pain and without suffering any real injury."

Sigmund Breitbart comes from a Jewish family long noted for its strength. To judge from such examples of physical strength and dexterity as the European Breitbart, and the display of muscular agility by American Jews like Benny Leonard and Harry Houdini, it looks as if a sturdier Jew is now in the making. The poor, despised Ghetto type with bent shoulders and hollow chest is rapidly passing. The Jews of today can point with pride to Sigmund Breitbart as the ideal presentment of their people from a physical standpoint just as Einstein typifies the Jewish ideal in the world of the intellect.

The Man With the Iron Jaw

Siegmund Breitbart, the Marvel

NEWSPAPERS all over the country have been full of the extraordinary feats of Siegmund Breitbart. Strong men and authorities on feats of strength have been puzzled to know how it is that Breitbart can bite through iron chains. Breitbart himself goes merrily on, performing his feats before vaudeville audiences, inviting all and sundry who care to come and examine for themselves each feat of strength that he performs.

Quite a few readers of HEALTH and LIFE have written in letters about this marvelous man. Several issues of HEALTH and LIFE have made references to his feats, so that Breitbart is not exactly a stranger to you. But, as promised earlier, I want to tell you a little bit more about him.

Breitbart is an enthusiast for the healthy, the strong, and the beautiful. He is, in other words, a physical culturist first, and then a Strong Man. It was his interest in the human body that led him to develop his enormous strength; for once upon a time Breitbart was a weakling, even a worry to his doctors. Determined not to be weak, he studied his body. As he grew up he studied all the physical culture courses he could get, bought every bit of physical culture apparatus he could lay his hands on, invented apparatus of his own, practised in every manner to investigate for himself the best laws of developing his body. As he himself says, "Strong Men are made, not born. Every man, young or old, should be strong. I know that every man can be strong if

he has the will and determination to take the simple necessary exercises. Therefore every man who is a weakling has been made so by himself alone; either by choice or through ignorance".

Breitbart is a Polish aristocrat and an intellectual. He is a musician, poet, writer, and thinker. But his love of the human body is so great that he has devoted his life to showing the world what a man can do with his body. There is more than just showmanship about his performances. He seeks to inspire those with whom he comes in contact with the same desires that fire him, and it is for this reason he has taken on this career, not only of showman, but of physical training expert. After all, if a man has done for himself what Breitbart has done, he has a right to pose as an authority and show how it can be done.

In his clothes Breitbart is not a ponderous looking man. He is so well proportioned that he looks more like a college athlete, and, of course, every inch an aristocrat. His measurements are as follows: Height, 5 ft. 1 in.; neck, 19 ins.; biceps, 18¾ ins.; forearm, 16 ins.; waist, 35 ins.; chest, 50 ins.; thigh, 26 ins.; calf, 17 ins.; weight, 225 lbs. So it is when you see him stripped that you realize what an extraordinary physical specimen he is.

He is certainly a man with an iron jaw, because he is the first man ever to bite chains through with his teeth. He has absolutely nothing in his mouth; it is simply by pure strength that he snaps the chains in two. Dentists have examined his mouth and all they find is that his teeth are about four times as thick as the average person's teeth. But it was discovered that the teeth have grown right down into the jaw bones themselves.

To give an example of his enormous jaw strength Breitbart has himself hitched to a wagon carrying sixty persons. Then he had a couple of heavy cartshorses with the bronces fixed to an attachment in his mouth, and the horses drew the wagon all over the city, Breitbart's jaw forming the connecting link between wagon and horses.

Twisting iron bands around his arm is child's play to Breitbart; he also bends iron bars into horseshoes. These bars are only ten inches long, and are a half-inch thick. The extreme shortness makes this a terrific test of strength. He has enormous supporting power. He allows automobiles to run over him, and in some of his feats he allows his body to form a bridge over which a pageant of horses and oxen are driven. In another supporting feat he has a merry-go-round

(Continued on Page 338)

SIEGMUND BREITBART
A close up showing the tape measure round Breitbart's wonderful arm.

THE MAN WITH THE IRON JAW

"The Bill Is a Wow!" Says Fay King of Reopening of Hippodrome

By FAY KING

We never knew how much we loved the Hippodrome until it looked like we were going to lose it!

But B. F. Albee, head of the Keith Vaudeville, came to the rescue and saved the famous show shop for all us kids, from seven to seventy, and Monday night we were all on hand to show our appreciation of the re-opening.

The bill is a wow!

There's Breitbart—a bird that can roll a railroad tie like a cigarette paper and lays back on a board full of sharp spikes and lets a parade of horses march across his chest! An electric iron is a bonbon to that baby,

and he bites through an iron chain like it was a link of weenies.

Breitbart is the big thrill with his feats of strength, and I like the kindly manner and dignity of the elderly gentleman who makes his announcements. When he asked someone in the audience to select the side of the chain Breitbart should break, I yelled out "left," and then Breitbart gave me a piece of the chain for luck.

I felt like a star in the show. His new motordrome stunt is a Wow! Inside the whole dome on his chest while two men on motorcycles rush around it. He's some boy!

From Pittsburgh Sun, November 3, 1923.

Modern Samson Shows Strength Feats

Officials of the Carnegie Steel Company from the Edgar Thomson works were excited over the proposal of Sigmund Breitbart, the Polish Hercules, to bend and break with his bare hands, bars, beams, and even rails made in the Braddock furnaces.

General Superintendent G. A. Hartman, John Lloyd, G. A. Balsinger and James Johnson, provided products of the steel works for this Modern Samson to try his strength upon. They sent a truck load of Edgar Thomson products to the Davis Theatre yesterday. Among the steel delivered and now on exhibition in the lobby are some steel rails, 130 pounds to the foot, beams, rods and flat steel. In addition, an immense chain used on the magnetic crane to lift the heaviest loads.

From N. Y. Telegraph, September 21, 1923.

Greatest Strong Man Delights Crowd

Breitbart, the Polish strong man who performs incredible feats of skill and showmanship requiring the power of a locomotive, broke the house record at the Orpheum Theatre last week. He became an idol of Brooklyn youth and the athletic clubs attended the Orpheum en masse.

The regular fans liked Breitbart from the first, for instead of weight lifting he did novel and sensational stunts with great skill and showmanship. He is as graceful as Jack Dempsey and moreover good looking. Breitbart did not forget the welcome from Dempsey who met him at the pier to be first a wire with his good wishes to the champion to the fans thousands on Friday night. Breitbart is a better showman than Sandow, and furthermore he has a greater and more interesting repertoire of stunts.

63. Breitbart in America – 4

STRONG MAN PLAYING AT KEITH'S THEATER

Sigmund Breitbart in Line of Samson and Sandow With Feats.

Since the days of Samson, remarkable feats of strength have always attracted the attention of the masses. Sandow was a popular idol for years and people traveled from great distances to see him perform.

During the past few years no man of great or supernatural strength had been discovered until one day a European scout for the variety halls of the continent heard of young Pole, the son of a blacksmith. The scout traveled to Lodz, Poland, where this boy had been the wonder of the surrounding country. He was quick to realize the possibilities and after much persuasion succeeded in making a contract with Sigmund Breitbart for a tour of Europe. As a result he has been the idol of every capital and has entertained wherever he appeared. The European scout for the B. F. Keith circuit saw him perform and started negotiations which ended in the signing of a contract for a tour of the Keith houses in the United States.

This remarkable tower of strength, appearing at Keith's this week, bends iron bars with his hands and teeth, working them into artistic scroll designs. He drives spikes through hard wood with his bare fists, bites tire chains in half with his teeth and supports the weight of a dozen men on a miniature merry-go-round on his chest. Probably his most sensational stunt is resting his bare back on a board of sharp-pointed nails while a mounted horse walks across his body on a runway.

On Tuesday afternoon in front of Keith's Theatre before more than 15,000 persons he performed probably the most unusual and sensational demonstration of strength ever witnessed in Washington.

He was chained to the seat of a truck. The horses were hitched to his teeth instead of the truck. The entire pull of the horses and weight of the truck and fifty men was sustained by his iron jaw. In this manner, the strange looking vehicle made its way from Keith's Theatre to F street, F to Fourteenth, Fourteenth to G street and G street back to Keith's entrance.

Siegmund Breitbart a Muscular Wonder and Puzzle.

Looks Like a College Athlete

Breitbart is one of the most unusual figures on the stage. He is nothing less than a muscular wonder. He is said to have baffled scientists in England, France and Poland—his homeland—who have tried in vain to explain the source of his almost miraculous powers.

Unlike the various Sandow and strong men that have loomed up on the foreign and American stages within the past ten years, Breitbart does not demonstrate his superhuman strength by lifting cumbersome objects, raising pianos from the floor or loading his powerful frame with eight or nine men larger than himself. These feats he can also call upon occasion. But he manipulates metal of every known degree of hardness, and there is in his performance no trace of chicanery or illusion. What he does he performs in plain sight of every one. He is a prodigy, for he works intimately, slowly and with little or no effort.

In appearance he resembles a college football hero rather than a professional entertainer.

Breitbart is Strongest Man in the World

Bites Through Tire Chains

Breitbart is the strongest man in the world and is also called "the best looking man in Europe," but he doesn't go in for weight lifting. He says that any man of muscle can pack big loads, so what he features is showmanship in sensational feats that none but he can perform. Breitbart takes angle irons and winds them like straw around his arm. He breaks thick pieces of iron and steel as the ordinary man breaks a match. He takes a five-inch spike and drives it with his bare hands up to the head in a heavy plank. He bites through tire chains, and with his jaw holds a steel bar from which six men hang on each side. He sits on a truck loaded with steel girders and holding a cable in his mouth has it connected with a motor which hauls the great load up to his teeth. Everything that Breitbart does is out in inspection and his claim preformed is that nothing is in the spotlight with a semblance from the audience to witness it. He simply has unusual strength and skill. He kept the audience awestruck and amazed throughout the entire performance.

64. Breitbart in America – 5

Breitbart Featured by the Leading Newspapers of America

"SUPERMAN OF THE AGES"

65. Breitbart's Headlines

BREITBART'S SAYINGS

by Siegmund Breitbart

Strength and health are the most valuable riches in life.

He who does not endeavor to become strong is a criminal against himself.

If you wish to be strong and healthy it behooves you not to neglect physical exercises.

No one should dodge exercising one's body.

It is never too late to start exercising one's body.

Everybody, no matter what his occupation, should take some time to exercise his body.

Emotional and mental exhaustion are result of physical exhaustion.

If you wish to avoid exhaustion - exercise your body.

Everybody can have strong and well-toned muscles, he simply has to want it.

Well-toned muscles are proof of strength of will and as such constitute the best security in life.

If you wish to have dependable muscles - exercise them.

If you wish to have broad shoulders, a high chest, a straight posture and strong arms and hands - exercise your body.

He who does not advance - regresses.

If you wish to advance - exercise your body.

Nobody is born strong, but everybody can become strong. He shall exercise his body.

When you are in low spirits and your health fails you – remember that you alone are responsible, you did not exercise your body (literally: train your musculature).

66. Zishe Breitbart's grave in Berlin

67. Zishe's signature floral design

BIBLIOGRAPHY

Siegel, Jerry, *The Creation of a Superhero*, unpublished manuscript, 1976, pp. 12-13.

Goldsmith, Arnold, *The Golem Remembered, 1909-1980: Variations of a Jewish Legend* (Wayne State University Press, 1981), p. 22

Gillerman, Sharon, *"Samson in Vienna: The Theaters of Jewish Masculinity," Jewish Social Studies 9:2* (Winter, 2003), p. 65.

Gillerman, Sharon, *"Strongman Siegmund Breitbart and Interpretations of the Jewish Body", in Michael Brenner and Gideon Reuveni, Emancipation Through Muscles: Jews and Sports in Europe* (Lincoln: University of Nebraska Press, 2006), 63.

"Breitbart, Modern Samson: First American Appearance of Jewish Superman", The American Hebrew, September 28, 1923, p. 497.

Winkler,Gisela, *Circus Busch Geschichte einer Manege in Berlin*, Berlin, 1998, p.41

von Paula Busch, Roman. *"Samson", Berliner Morgenpost,* July 24-Septeber 2, 1923.

Mosse, George, *The Image of Man. The Creation of Modern Masculinity.* New York, 1996

Ilustrowany Kurier Codzienny roczniki z lat 1925 – 1926.

Akta stanu cywilnego miast Stryków i Łódz , Archiwum Państwowe w Łodzi

Breitbart, Siegmund, *Power Muscle*, New York, 1924.

Gauding, Daniela; Breitbart, Siegunt Sische, *Eisenkönig stürkster Mann der Welt: Breitbart Versus Hanussen*, 2006.

Gordon, Mel; Andrae, Thomas, *Siegel and Shuster`s Funnyman the first Jewish Superhero, from the Creators of Superman*, Feral House, U.S. Los Angeles, 2010.

Pinkas, Unger Awrom, *Moje miasteczko Stryków, wybór, tłumaczenie i opracowanie Monika Polit*, Stryków 2013.

Tye, Larry, *Superman*, Random House, University of Nebraska, U.S., Lincoln 2013.

Kaplan, Arie, *From Krakow to Krypton: Jews and Comic Books*, Philadelphia 2008.

Fingeroth, Danny, *Disguised as Clark Kent: Jews, Comics, and the Creation of the Superhero*, New York 2007.

Weinstein, Simcha, *Up Up and Oy Vey: How Jewish History, Culture and Values Shopped the Comic Book Superhero* (2006).

Gauding, Daniela; Breitbart, Siegmunt Sische. *Eisenkönig stärkster Mann der Welt: Breitbart Versus Hanussen* (2006).

Brenner, Michael; Devrem, Gideon. *Emancipation Through Muscles: Jews and Sports in Europe*, (2006).

Prager, Brad. *The Cinema of Werner Herzog*, (2007)

Gillerman, Sharon; Baader, Benjamin. *Jewish Masculinities: German Jews, Gender, and History*, (2012)

On YouTube, you can watch the material titled *Superman from Stryków*, in which Jacek Perzyński talks about the strong man. This channel has a series of videos about Zishe Breitbart has also been published by Gary Bart in cooperation with The Yiddish Book Center. You can also watch other films (search for *Zishe Breitbart*) dedicated to the strongman, who show fragments of his original shows as well as people explaining why he was the genesis for Superman. Information about the author on the last or penultimate page of the book:

A collection of documents, articles and illustrations from various years of the Twentieth Century including the private resources of Gary Bart.

ABOUT THE AUTHOR

Jacek Perzyński is a researcher in the history of her most unknown and mysterious history. His books or press articles published in Poland aroused many discussions about the topics he touched upon. In this publication he proves where Superman came from and who was his progenitor. All interested in this subject, the author asks for contact at the following e-mail address: *jacekper75@o2.pl*

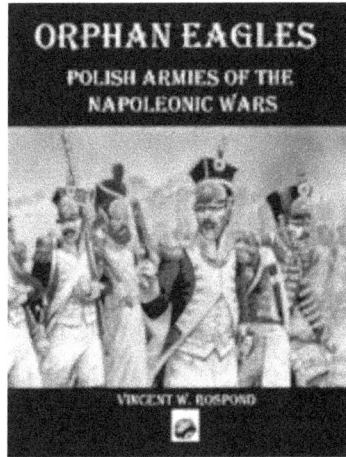

Look for more books from Winged Hussar Publishing, LLC/Pike & Powder
– E-books, paperbacks and Ltd Edition hardcovers.
The best in history, science fiction and fantasy at:

www.wingedhussarpublishing.com

or follow us on Facebook at:

Winged Hussar Publishing LLC

Or on twitter at:

WingHusPubLLC

For information and upcoming publications

www.ingramcontent.com/pod-product-compliance
Lightning Source LLC
Chambersburg PA
CBHW020937090426
42736CB00010B/1169